CITIZENSHIP,
The Community,
AND PUBLIC SERVICE

HARVEY K. NEWMAN

Kendall Hunt
publishing company

Cover image © Shutterstock

Kendall Hunt
publishing company

www.kendallhunt.com
Send all inquiries to:
4050 Westmark Drive
Dubuque, IA 52004-1840

Copyright © 2010 by Harvey K. Newman

ISBN 978-0-7575-7745-1

Printed in the United States of America
10 9 8 7 6 5 4 3 2

CONTENTS

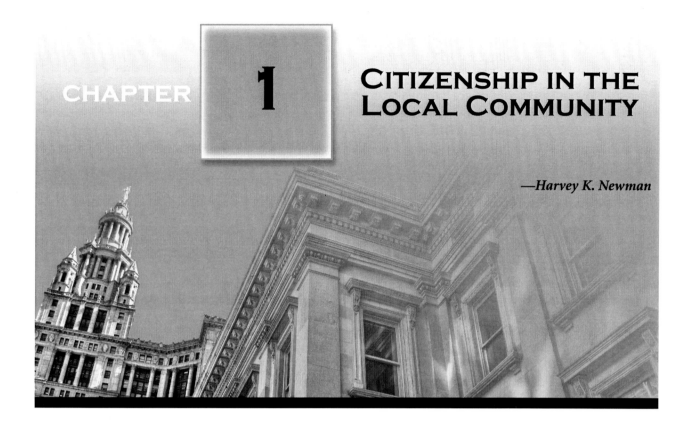

CHAPTER 1

CITIZENSHIP IN THE LOCAL COMMUNITY

—Harvey K. Newman

"Citizenship, the community, and the public service" is an interesting combination of words. No doubt we have used the word citizenship for much of our lives. In most people's minds that concept refers to the relationship between an individual and the government, usually at the national or state level. A great deal of effort is made during our early years to teach young people in schools the importance of citizenship in the state and nation. Each class day in most schools begins with the students reciting together the pledge of allegiance to the United States of America. As students get older they are also taught to be good citizens of the state in which they reside. Growing up in the state of North Carolina, every student was required in the eighth grade to learn that state's song, motto, government, and history. For the same reason, most high school and college students must learn about the structure and operation of the U.S. government.

This education for state and national citizenship serves an important purpose. Students are taught to understand that, as citizens, they have both rights and responsibilities. Among the rights, citizens may vote and hold public office. The responsibilities include paying taxes, serving on a jury, obeying the laws, and defending the country, if required to do so. Thus, we grow up with an understanding of citizenship, within the state and the nation, but with little attention to our local community. This is the objective of this book—to teach you about your role as a citizen in the community. It is to help you learn what you need to know to be an effective citizen of your local government.

Why is this important? One answer might be that the activities of local government are the most important in determining the quality of a person's life. Public safety—police, fire, and emergency services are critical in the protection of your life and property. A safe and sanitary water supply is necessary to keep you healthy. Trash removal and sewer lines help to keep your immediate environment free from disease and the threat of infections (not to mention less odor). Streets, sidewalks, and bike paths are part of the public works that provide access to jobs, schools, and shopping, as well as exercise. City parks are available for recreation and as places for people to gather. Old buildings need to be closed up and perhaps even demolished, while permits must be issued to build or improve newer ones. Local governments also provide schools. While other levels of government may be involved in paying for some of these municipal services, it is a local government, either city or county, that provides the services that most directly affect the quality of our daily lives. Yet, we usually take these services for granted until we experience a broken sewer pipe, or a pothole in the street, or some other breakdown in our local services.

There is another reason citizens need to understand their local community. A long-time member and Speaker of the U.S. House of Representatives, Thomas "Tip" O'Neil, often said that "All politics is local." O'Neil understood this to mean that in deciding issues involving the nation or even the world, he tried to imagine how the decision would affect the people in his old neighborhood in North Cambridge, Massachusetts. O'Neil realized that the political process in the Boston area had made it possible for poor Irish immigrants and their children to improve their lives by providing access to housing, jobs and all the things that are taken for granted as part of the "American way of life." Even though we may hear more about state and national politics as we watch the news, the most important issues that affect people's lives are the local ones.

So, if the local community is the area that has the most direct impact on the quality of a person's life, why don't more people care about it and take part as active citizens of their local government? Perhaps when they realize how important it is, they do begin to take part. When people know more about their local government, how it fits into their lives, and how to be an engaged citizen, then, the result could be better communities with more people participating in the public service. That brings up the third group of words in the title of this book— the public service. One of the goals of the course, that is part of a larger degree program, is to prepare students to enter the public service in either government or nonprofit organizations. This book is regarded as an initial step down this path. The hope is that the requirements for this course will lead you toward a meaningful career in public service. But, what if one's path does not follow the trail of employment in either the public or the nonprofit sectors? Has it been a waste of time to learn about citizenship, the community, and the public service? No matter how you chose to earn your living after you complete your degree, we hope that you will be a good citizen. If you take an active part in the affairs of your neighborhood, your town, county, or other local community, you will also be more likely to do your part in the life of your state and nation. Perhaps we will have prepared you to think globally, but to act locally. We firmly believe that O'Neil was right when he said, "All politics is local." Citizenship may be, also.

How do we begin learning about citizenship in the community and the public service? A good first step is to realize that each of us owes some sense of loyalty to our community. We are citizens of our local community, and, as such, we have both rights and responsibilities at this level. Conditioned as we are to think of citizenship as a requirement of our state and national governments, we may have to "un-do" quite a few years of history.

It is difficult to imagine, but if schools such as ours existed in ancient Athens, young students might have begun their day by reciting together the Athenian Oath of Citizenship. They would have said:

> We will ever strive for the ideals
>
> and sacred things of the city,
>
> both alone and with many;
>
> we will unceasingly seek to quicken
>
> the sense of public duty;
>
> we will revere and obey the city's laws;
>
> we will transmit this city
>
> not only not less, but greater,
>
> better, and more beautiful
>
> than it was transmitted to us.

Fast forward more than 2,000 years to the present, and it is difficult to conceive that a large metropolitan area would have an oath of citizenship. We have almost no sense of municipal citizenship. We lack an awareness of the need "to strive for the ideals" of the city. Among the diverse population who might call any city in the United States home, getting agreement on how to "transmit this city... greater, better, and more beautiful than it was transmitted to us" is a challenge. For example, consider the task of getting approval for the installation of a piece of public art. As anyone who has ever faced this challenge quickly learns the task of getting agreement on what is beautiful among even a relatively few individuals is daunting. Consider for a moment a recent case of public art in the City of Chicago. The mayor and civic leaders were seeking to transform an old air strip into a new lakefront park. As a showpiece of public art for the new, Millennium Park these leaders commissioned an artist named Anish Kapoor, who enjoyed an international reputation, to produce a sculpture for the site. The artist described his objectives for the work in these words, "What I wanted to do in Millennium Park is make something that would engage the Chicago skyline... so that one will see the clouds kind of floating in, with those very tall buildings reflected in the work. And then, since it is in the form of a gate, the participant, the viewer, will be able to enter into this very deep chamber that does, in a way, the same thing to one's reflection as the exterior of the piece is doing to the reflection of the city around." The result was a huge work of art weighing 110 tons that was 66 feet long and 33 feet high made of polished, reflective steel. The name given to the work by the artist was the Cloud Gate (Millennium Park, Art and Architecture, City of Chicago web site). When it was initially unveiled to the public in 2005, many did not like the sculpture saying it was a waste of money. Even those who liked the sculpture, called it "the Bean," as the finished Cloud Gate looks like a giant chrome bean. As more and more people walked past it (or under it) and touched it, as well as saw changing reflections in the shiny surface, they began to embrace the Bean. It is now regarded as an object of civic pride, in much the same way that residents of Paris gradually came to embrace the Eiffel Tower. Hardly anyone knows it by its official name as everyone just calls it the Bean. Before and during its construction, Chicago residents would probably not have approved the design or the expenditure for this new piece of public art. Agreement that its design was attractive and that it seems perfect for the site in the new park would have been impossible to get if the matter were put to a vote. Hardly anyone except the mayor and a few civic leaders would have been able to agree that this sculpture would make the city more beautiful than before. While this example of public art turned out well, it illustrates the difficulty of getting agreement about illusive ideas of what is attractive among the large, diverse population of a major city.

The next question to consider is how can we "quicken the sense of public duty" among urban residents who are often not aware that they have any obligations to the local community in which they live? This book is designed to address this task of preparing urban dwellers to understand their roles as citizens in the local community.

The first task is to understand how our system of government is designed to work. What does the well-informed citizen need to know about the federal system? The U.S Constitution does not mention cities, but it established the federal government and set up the framework in which states and cities exist. The constitution gives certain roles to the national government and reserves other powers for the states. In turn, the states create local governments that in most places include both county and municipal governments. An effective citizen of the local community must know the place of his or her local government within the federal system.

Perhaps the next question that a citizen might raise is what does my local government do? One of the most important aspects of local government is what is collectively known as "public works." This is how a city maintains itself. Public works includes paving streets and fixing pot holes, keeping the water pure for drinking and treating sewage before it is discharged, managing the zoning code, collecting trash, maintaining parks, and many more services that citizens depend upon.

Next, a citizen needs to understand the structure of local government. People often ask, why can't the mayor fire a department head in the local government such as the parks and recreation department director whose actions are drawing criticism? The answer is in the city charter or other document that creates the structure of the local government. In one form of local government the city council hires the department heads, who do the day-to-day work of the community. Within this type of city governmental structure, the mayor cannot fire the parks and recreation director, since this person reports to the entire city council. In another common form of local government, the mayor and members of the council hire a city manager, who has the authority to hire the department heads such as the police chief. Under this structure the mayor is not individually responsible for hiring (or firing) any individual who works in the local government. This can cause confusion among local residents when they are unhappy with some aspect of their government. In a recent example, citizens in a small town started a campaign to remove their mayor from office by means of a re-call election. The action by angry and well-intentioned citizens was misplaced since the city manager was the one who caused the problems and angered the public. In the end, citizens of this community felt even more frustrated because they felt they were not able to make a difference by removing the official responsible for their anger. How could the residents of this town have expressed their anger more effectively? One way is for citizens to understand the structure of their local government in order to be effective in making changes.

Even after a person understands the structure of their local government, there are other questions that must be answered. How are decisions really made within the community? Does the mayor tell the parks and recreation department head to keep the city's recreation centers open later in the evening and expect to have the decision obeyed? Can a business leader meet with the department head over a cup of coffee and make the city official understand how critical it is to keep the costs of operating local government lower by closing the recreation centers instead of keeping them open longer? If the department head understands how interested business leaders are in this decision, will the recreation centers remain closed in order to save money and keep taxes low? What about the role of a group of neighborhood residents who feel that having additional hours for the recreation center will keep young people occupied after school and less likely to get into trouble? Whose voice will be more important in making the decision? Often it is the informal ways of making decisions in a community that tell us more about how to get something done than the formal structure of local government. Knowledge about this informal decision making in a community can make an individual a more effective citizen.

Suppose that you are trying to make a difference in your community by going down to a food bank in order to volunteer for a few hours each week. Will working in a nonprofit organization such as the community food bank help you to become a better citizen? Taking part in civic activities such as the Parent Teacher Association (PTA), the neighborhood homeowners association, or the food bank no doubt builds a set of skills that can be useful to an individual. This process is sometimes called the development of social capital. But, does being a good volunteer in a civic activity build social capital that helps you be more effective in the political life of your community? Opinion on these questions is divided. On the one hand, perhaps the civil sector is separate from the political, so that the skill set you acquire in one setting does not help you as you try to influence policies in the political arena. The other view is that the social capital from one sector enables the citizen to bridge actions in the nonprofit world into public life. Perhaps by being an active member of a local school's PTA, an individual learns more about what is going on inside a particular school and what the needs of the school's students, teachers, and administrators might be. Does this knowledge increase the likelihood that the PTA participant is going to lobby the school board or other public body for increased support for the school? This is at the heart of the debate over the role of a citizen who participates in a civic activity and the development of social capital that makes this individual a more effective participant in the political life of the community.

Finally, what are some of the roles that an individual citizen might play in order to make changes in the local community? Consider two examples: first, it is a rare person who has walked down the street of a major city and not been asked for change by a stranger. Reaching into a pocket or purse to give to a person in need is an example of one-to-one, direct assistance. This type of assistance may (or may not) directly benefit the individual, but will do little to change the larger system of policies provided by the network of public and nonprofit agencies working to improve the lives of those in need. On the other hand, attending a city council meeting and speaking in support of more food for homeless people will have less direct impact on the life of the person who asks us for change, but it has more potential to change the policies in place that address the needs of large numbers of individuals.

When a citizen asks the question, what can be done to influence change in my community, there are a variety of activities that can lead to change. Some, like the first example above, are more likely to impact individuals in need and have little impact on change in the system of policies affecting larger numbers of people. Other actions may have more potential to change policies, but less impact on individuals in need. There are also a variety of ways in which citizens can influence change. These range from voting and campaign support at the most basic level to protest and confrontation. Another possible way to make change in the community is to run for office. The array of ways for citizens to influence change must be part of the skill set of a well-informed resident.

These are some of the issues and questions that are addressed in this book. Will all of this knowledge and skills make you a good citizen of your local community? The answer is probably not without practice. Citizenship is not a spectator sport, but an activity that demands you take an active part. An initial step toward this is through civic engagement. There is no substitute for learning about what is going on in your community by becoming a participant as a volunteer in a nonprofit or public agency. However, simply showing up at the agency setting a few hours per week is no guarantee of making a significant contribution to the community or of learning from the experience. How can these two goals be balanced? One way is through service learning, which is a process for teaching and learning that depends upon students reflecting upon the experiences they are having as volunteers in the community. Service learning in a public or nonprofit organization provides an initial step in career development for some students and for the education of everyone for their roles of a citizen.

At the conclusion of the semester, will students stand and recite a pledge of allegiance to their local community? Perhaps not, but here is what we hope to achieve: We hope that you and others with you will strive for the ideals of the city. In the process we hope you will quicken your sense of public duty by having a better understanding of what is expected of you as a citizen. We trust that, even if you do not revere the laws of your local government, you will obey them. Finally, we hope you will want to pass on the city in which you live as a better (and perhaps even a more beautiful) place for those who come after you. These are our goals for you as citizens in the community and the public service.

CHAPTER 1
Citizenship in the Local Community

1. Select two examples of public art (i.e., artwork that is available and visible to the public) in your community or a nearby locality. In the space provided, describe the two pieces of art. Compare the descriptions you have written with those of others in the class. Can you agree on what makes each one attractive or not? If there is disagreement on how you regard the examples of public art, how might these disagreements make it difficult to purchase new works for public display?

2. Draft the wording for a revised "Oath of Local Citizenship" for your community.

3. Describe some of the reasons you believe that taking part as a volunteer in service-learning will make you a better citizen of your community.

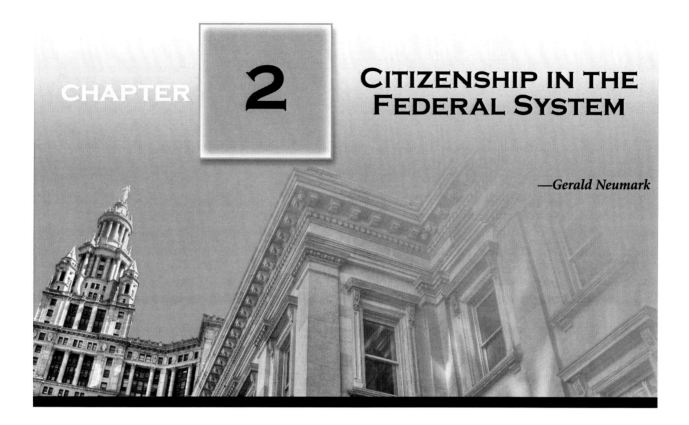

CHAPTER 2 CITIZENSHIP IN THE FEDERAL SYSTEM

—Gerald Neumark

When you run a red light and are pulled over, whose law have you broken? Did you break a federal law? A state law? A city or county law? There is no simple answer. It really depends on whether you are on a local residential street, a U.S. highway, State Route 29, or even driving in a national park. Does the President of the United States, the chief executor of the law of this nation, have the authority to give you the ticket for your offense? What about the governor? Which layer of government has the most authority related to this issue?

How do local governments fit into all of these questions? Or as Phillips (2010) puts it: "Who runs this town"? (450) The answers relate to one concept: federalism. Thus, to understand fully the role of local governments in this nation, including their abilities and limitations, one must have a full appreciation of the nature of the U.S. federal system.

Cities in the United States are not independent although there is no mention (or definition) of them in the Constitution (Saltzenstein et al., 2008, 159). To begin with they are nothing more than creations of their individual states. As such, they must follow a whole list of laws and policies which come from our state and federal governments. We, as citizens, in turn must obey the laws, ordinances, and policies of all levels of government. Ironically, "the biggest news stories about the public sector often focus on the federal government. . . our daily lives. . . are profoundly affected by the ordinary activities of state and local governments" (Bluestone et al., 2008, 287). Thus, in spite and because of the limitations imposed by the U.S. federal system it is important to study this country's local governments within this context.

FEDERALISM DEFINED

We begin our exploration by establishing an understanding of what federalism is not as it relates to local governments. Cities in the United States are not directly controlled by the government in Washington, DC. This is different than in a *unitary* system where local governments are subdivisions of a national entity.

Unitary governments are found in such nations as France, Argentina, Israel, Jordan, and Nigeria. In these nations, it is the national governments that determine the operations of their local governments. "Local governments can be altered or even abolished by the national government acting alone" (Dye, 2008, 272). In addition, there are no states or established provinces with political authority in such systems. France provides an example. If the French parliament wishes to change the city council structure of *Toulouse*, they simply act to do so. Interestingly, Paris is the only city in France with its own police department. The remainder of the local governments is under the jurisdiction of the national police force.

The French case is much different than what one finds in our country. A quick look at downtown Atlanta, Georgia provides a telling example of the many layers of government affecting one city. Within the downtown area one can find the following police agencies: on the national level the Federal Protective Service; on the state level one can see the Georgia State Patrol, the Georgia Bureau of Investigation, the Georgia State University police, the Georgia Capitol police, the World Congress Center police, and the MARTA transit police. On the county level, the Fulton County Sheriff's Department as well as the Fulton County Police has their own jurisdiction. And on the local level there is the Atlanta City Police Department. Perhaps all of these policing agencies may seem excessive, but they certainly exist within and are nurtured by our federal system.

What then is federalism? Is it something more than just a web of governmental duplication? From the above examples, it should be clear that a federal system implies different layers of government having authority over the execution of policies and laws that affect our everyday lives. Each of these levels has their own sphere of *separate* and *autonomous* authority. DiIulio defines federalism as a political system in which the local units of government, as well as a national government can make final authoritative decisions and whose existence is protected in law (1998, 52). Waste agrees: federalism, as practiced in the United States is "the division of government authority into national and sub-national units with each unit having a genuine measure of authority" (1998, 183; also see Peterson, 1981, 67). Elizar presents a bit more comprehensive definition: Federalism "is the mode of political organization that unites smaller politics [political units] within an overarching political system by distributing power among general and constituent governments in a manner designed to protect the existence and authority of both national and sub-national political systems enabling all to share in the overall systems decision-making and executive processes" (1966, 2).

Notice the common thread that runs through all of these definitions: all governments on all levels have power, authority, independence, and protection under the law. A quick look at any American city and many local political units of all types shows the operative nature of these definitions. So many governments, each having a piece of the action! But, why? We now turn to that question.

WHY FEDERALISM?

Wouldn't it be easier if our national government simply exercised control over its cities? (Don't they seem to do so now anyway?) Why all these different levels, duplications, complexities, and complications? The quick answer is for our protection; born out of the colonial mistrust of government on all levels. Our federal system, as designed by the Framers of the Constitution, serves to discourage any single powerful faction from dominating the body politic. With such a system, James Madison believed that, "Majority factions were unlikely to form in a large and diverse republic, since the number and diversity of interests in the nation prevented a single faction from gaining control of the federal government" (Gais and Fossett, 2005, 488). A federal system institutionalized this decentralization of power and authority.

Not only were the Framers concerned about factions, however. There was also a skepticism regarding individuals within the government itself, acting in their own self-interest and not for the good of the population. Thus, such a federal system sets up competition: "Governments and government officials can be constrained by competition with other governments and other government officials" (Dye, 1990, 2–3). A unitary system facilitates powerful inner governmental factions, and self-interested government officials could very well result in the usurpation of control over our local governments: in a sense a local oligarchy. Competition among 83,000 local governments in this country prevents this from taking place. (For a complete understanding of the Framer's conceptions supporting governmental competition see the Federalist Paper 10.)

In addition to protection, federalism fits neatly into the American philosophy of checks and balances; the operation of which may be seen as a function of so many "national" programs mandating the implementation and further policy development authority to state and local officials. "Federalism ensures that policy-making does not consist of the federal government commanding and states and communities automatically snapping to attention (Press and Yerburg, 1983, 22). Such mandates insure that policy making is multilevel, a two-way street. It is through the implementation process that local governments are able to provide a check regarding national and state government demands. Being put into this position gives our cities a sense of legitimacy and responsibility not found in a unitary system. American cities are indeed an important cog in the entire policy-making process.

There is also an important American cultural value inherent in federalism: the tradition of local control. Our local government is our closest and most accessible government. By far, the majority of the rules and regulations American citizens face on an everyday basis come down from our local governments. These range from our children's education to our use of private or public transportation. Take a minute and think about how many local ordinances you had to follow on your way to school today. How well does the Secretary of Housing and Urban Affairs know your neighborhood and its concerns? Or even your governor? How well does your member of city council or county commissioner know this information?

Even though such councils exist in unitary systems, urban policy is still dictated from the top. In addition to policy is access. Once again, how easy is it for you to travel to Washington, DC for an appointment with the HUA secretary? Is it more difficult than seeing your member of council or county commissioner? The answers to these questions are obvious.

We are a nation of 300 million individuals. We all have our demands on government. How can government address these demands, keep our diversity rich and intact, protect us and allow us to petition our government? The federal system as constructed in the United States may be awkward; however, it is the most effective way that all of its governments can accomplish the concerns brought about in such a large and diverse nation. With an understanding of what American federalism is and why it exists, we now turn to the questions of how its present variant developed and what is the role of local governments within this system.

THE EVOLUTION OF AMERICAN FEDERALISM

Federalism today is very different as envisaged by the Framers. Because of the colonial experience with British dominance, the newly formed American state desired a weak central government; however, in just five years after the signing of the Treaty of Paris, this proved to be untenable. A strong central government was not only inevitable, it was necessary. The question then became how do we create a stronger central government and yet keep the states as sovereign as possible? To this end, the Framers created a state centered federal system. Each entity had their separate sphere of authority. One level could not infringe upon the authority of the other. Although the Supremacy Clause of the Constitution gave the national government ultimate power in case of conflict, it was understood that the national government would not interfere with the workings of the state governments. State governments were thought of as the primary government for Americans. The first understanding of our federal system was that it was not merely decentralized government. Beyond simple decentralization, our system was much more concerned with intergovernmental relations (Dye, 1990, 4). This early constitutional philosophy permitted the people to decide which level of government—national, state, or local is most likely to enact the policy they prefer (Dye, 2008, 275). In this period the state government clearly won out. State centered federalism worked reasonably well for about 80 years.

Then came the American Civil War. One of the results of that war was the realization that states were not as supreme and definitely not as sovereign as was conceived in the early years of the Constitution. It was the Civil War that transformed our country from a nation of states to a nation. While the power and authority of states diminished, the power and authority of the national government increased to the point that a new conception of federalism emerged: duel federalism (1865–1913). Although each level still had its own jurisdictional realm, power and authority were now equally divided. This more balanced conception of federalism lasted for about fifty years.

The year 1913 saw a major shift in power. This was the year of the adoption of the 16th Amendment to the Constitution, the establishment of the income tax. The 16th Amendment represented a shift to the beginning of dominant national authority. Incomes generated within a state could be collected by the federal government. Although it was the states that ratified the Amendment, it was clear that at least on this important policy issue the national government dominated. States could not bar Washington from collecting this tax.

This federal dominance found its culmination in Great Depression and World War II acts. Power and authority could no longer be considered duel. The national government became clearly dominant. Through grants in aid the federal government was able to induce the states into 'cooperation' which ranged from joint execution of some policies such as welfare to federally mandated implementation of others. For the states refusing to cooperate, federal funds became less available. This cooperative federalism lasted from 1913 to 1964.

President Lyndon Johnson's Great Society policies introduced a new conception of federalism. By the advent of these programs starting in 1964, power now firmly rested in the hands of the national government. This new centralized federalism essentially rendered the 10th Amendment meaningless. (In regards to the 10th Amendment issue, see the discussion of *Garcia v. the San Antonio Metropolitan Transit Authority* below.) Starting with the Great Society Program, the federal government directly intervened into previously held state policy authority. The role of states and local governments shifted to that of implementing national policies. Centralized federalism lasted to about 1980.

A short-lived variant of federalism came about in 1972. This was President Richard Nixon's "New Federalism." Nixon's idea was to reverse the policy flow created by Johnson during the centralized federalism period. Under this new federalism funds were to flow directly back to state and local governments giving them a much greater amount of flexibility in the determination of policy development and implementation. Such policies as Urban Development Action Grants (UDAG grants), Urban Mass Transportation Administration grants (UMTA), and General Revenue Sharing became an important part of national, state and local intergovernmental relations during this period of time. This philosophy, however, changed once Nixon left office in 1974. President Ford followed by President Carter slowly moved away from UDAG and revenue sharing. Thus the concept behind new federalism, increased local policy development autonomy, was replaced by block grants which are still in effect today.

One final note: Although President Reagan also termed his intergovernmental relations policies "New Federalism," the Reagan conception was very different than Nixon's. Under President Reagan many particularly social policies were shifted from the federal to state and local governments. Many of these social programs came in the form of unfunded mandates, putting a direct financial burden on state and local governments. The term New Federalism, then, has a very opposite meaning depending whether or not we are viewing the policies of Presidents Richard Nixon or Ronald Reagan.

We are currently in a period coined by some political scientists as "coercive federalism." (Dye, 2008, 279) As mentioned above, the 10th Amendment was assumed to be dead during the period of centralized federalism. In a very real sense, the 1985 Supreme Court decision in *Garcia v. San Antonio Metropolitan Transit Authority* put the nail in the coffin. The court ruled that the transit authority, a local government, must pay overtime to its workers in the same way as if it were a private business organization. Thus, the ruling said that Congress had the right to legislate certain rules and regulations for local governments (Hall, 1999, 99–100; also see Padover, 1995, 94–102). This ruling had the effect of giving the national government the ability to determine local policy in direct opposition to the intention of the 10th Amendment. As an outgrowth of *Garcia*, the national government established a number of local preemption policies including the American with Disabilities Act, Title IX of the Aid to Education Act, and Title VI of the Civil Rights Act, which provided parameters for how local policies are formulated and carried out with respect to public and private discriminatory practices (Dobbins, 2009, 265). Up until this point the authority to develop and implement such policies would have been up to state and local governments.

Has federalism become a one-way street? Are we approaching becoming a unitary system? Even if this were not the case, there are implications for the ability of local governments to establish their own policies and laws.

At the very least, local governments must exist within the new realities of federalism: they must play in a whole new ball field.

The seeds of modern federalism were planted in the Constitution itself. Three clauses: the Supremacy Clause, the Commerce Clause, and the Necessary and Proper Clause have served to make the federal government supreme in all matters. Add the dependency of cities on the largess of the federal government to the clauses and one finds the structure of modern federalism. A brief definition of the three clauses is in order.

The Supremacy Clause states that in all matters between and among the different levels of government, the federal government shall remain supreme. Any city act or ordinance, including the city charter itself must not be in conflict with the U.S. Constitution. As mentioned above, for example, a local government cannot negate any portion of Title IX.

The Commerce Clause, "gives Congress the power to regulate commerce with foreign nations, and among several states, and with Indian Tribes" (Lorch, 2001, 27). Taken at face value, one may ask what this clause has to do with local government. However, since almost everything produced in this nation crosses state lines (including purchases by local governments), it gives the federal government that much more control over the authority of local governmental policies. For example, a city does not have the right to regulate the sale of over-the-counter drugs within its jurisdiction.

Finally, the Necessary and Proper Clause allows the federal government to make whatever laws are necessary and proper to carry out its various powers (Lorch, 2001, 23). It should be clear to even a casual observer that the broad nature of this clause gives the federal government an open door to not only establish local government policy but to preempt some policies already in place.

Indeed Waste suggested that because of all the federal mandates, preemptions and regulations imposed upon local governments, cities have become nothing more than colonies of the national government, creating a neo-colonial system of dependency (Waste, 1998, 183). Whether one agrees with this assessment or not, it is clear that cities operate within a rather restrictive environment ultimately created by not only the federal system per se, but dynamic conceptions defining the shift in roles among the national government, the states and the American cities. We now turn to another complicating factor in the U.S. federal structure, the role of the state as it relates to local governments.

Local Governments and the States

In spite of the fact that the United States does not have a unitary governmental system, U.S. cities are hardly independent. "Local governments owe their legal existence to their respective states. . . . A great deal of their legal status depends upon the acts of their state legislatures" (Press and Verberg, 1983, 121). There are also important local governmental policies and functions that are, for the most part, controlled by the state through mandated rules. These include transportation, environmental protection, and housing and urban development (Dobbins, 2009, 254). This is in addition to all of the federal restrictions and preemptions. The result is a great amount of uncertainty over the relationship between states and their cities.

This relationship begins with "home rule." Although the term home rule is applied everywhere in the United States to the ability of local political units to govern themselves independently, the real meaning of home rule varies from state to state. In some states, for example, cities with home rule have absolutely no protection against state interference in local policy-making. The states themselves have been uncertain and in constant flux as to how to treat their local governments. On the one hand, one finds that in some states, the state has ceded to their municipal governments a broad range of functional powers. On the other hand, some states have insisted that local governments carry the state policies in very specific ways. Indeed, this even happens within states in regards to different municipalities (Press and Verberg, 1983, 119). In all cases, regardless of the state's interpretation of home rule, state governments are still very much involved in the affairs of their local governments. If nothing else, states are becoming increasingly active in coordinating the policy outcomes of all the local governments within their jurisdictions (Press and Verberg, 1983, 24). All of this means that local governments, vis-à-vis the states, are in a very precarious position. They do not operate in a vacuum: far from it. Every policy and ordinance established and implemented by local governments must be considered within the context of the rights of other municipalities as well as their own position within the state.

Not only does home rule and state legislative authority determine the status and abilities of local governments, so does the state's purse strings. Only 4 percent of local budgets comes from the national government. The vast majority of local funds flow from the state. For the most part, they are not allowed to raise their own revenue, or they can only do so under severe restrictions: "The one thing that all cities have in common is the fact that they operate under state laws dictating how they may raise money" (Judd and Swanstrom, 2008, 306). This dependence on the largess of the state allows the state legislatures to impose even further restrictions on the operation of their cities. Perhaps it is accurate to say that in many parts of the United States, particularly in the Southeast, Waste's statement may be correct: local governments are more akin to colonies of their states. As with a colony, in many cases, the state draws out a great deal more in revenue from its larger cities than is distributed back through financial support and services. For years, the city government of Atlanta, Georgia has complained about precisely that: tax revenue collected in Georgia's most populated city has been redistributed back to smaller municipalities throughout the state. Atlanta sees a much smaller proportion of this revenue than would be the case if the city were able to retain the revenue collected within its city limits.

Whether or not one looks at legislative authority, home rule, or revenue disbursement, it is clear that local/state intergovernmental relations are a product of the U.S. federal system. The very ability of a city to exist flows from this system.

IMPLICATIONS AND CONCLUSION

"Municipal governments are located at the *bottom* [emphasis mine] of a three-tiered federal system of governance" (Judd and Swanstrom, 2008, 305). However, the role of the federal government vis-à-vis local government should not be overstated. Local governments do have rights and authority, albeit not constitutional. These rights and authority are simply limited. Whatever a local government does (policy) must be understood in the context of the constraints imposed by a federal system. "Their [local governments] place in the U.S. intergovernmental system basically limits their freedom to maneuver" (Judd and Swanstrom, 2008, 305). The increasing amount of federal mandates, often unfunded, imposes greater restrictions on local governmental policy choices (Gais and Fossett, 2005, 505). Added to this are the restrictions imposed by the various states, and one can see a system of severely constrained local governments. It is within this context that any study of urban governments must be understood. Cities are not helpless, just limited in their scope of policy formulation and operations. The good news is that it is truly amazing that U.S. cities are able to do as much as they are able to do.

Federalism is here to stay. No one can predict the future, but for the moment, the state government but particularly the national governments' role vis-à-vis local government is growing and changing, will continue to do so: "The national government has grown in power not only because the nation has grown in size and population, but also because we have become less a collection of isolated states and more a single nation. The words of the Constitution remain the same, but the reality to which the words apply has changed" (Lorch, 2001, 24). In spite of these changes, the Unites States is not heading toward a French-style unitary governmental structure. Thus, it is within the understanding of a federal system that we as students of urban studies must view the history, background, realities, and functioning of the American city. These limitations and possibilities make the study of cities all the more intriguing.

REFERENCES

Bluestone, Barry, Mary Huff, and Russell Williams. 2008. *The Urban Experience Economics, Society, And Public Policy*. New York: Oxford University Press.

Dobbins, Michael. 2009. *Urban Design and People*. Hoboken, NJ: John Wiley & Sons, Inc.

Dye, Thomas R. 1990. *American Federalism Competition Among Governments*. Lexington, MA: Lexington Books D. C. Heath and Company.

Dye, Thomas R. 2008. *Understanding Public Policy*, 12th edition. Upper Saddle River, NJ: Pearson Prentice Hall.

Elizar, Daniel J. 1966. *American Federalism: a View from the States*. New York: Thomas Y. Crowell.

Gais, Thomas and James Fossett. 2005. Joel D. Aberbach and Mark A. Peterson (Editors). *Institutions of American Democracy the Executive Branch*. New York: Oxford University Press.

Hall, Kermit L. (Editor). 1999. *The Oxford Guide to United States Supreme Court Decisions*. New York: Oxford University Press.

Judd, Dennis R. and Todd Swanstrom. 2008. *City Politics the Political Economy of Urban America*, 6th edition. New York: Pearson Longman.

Lorch, Robert S. *State & Local Politics the Great Entanglement*, 6th edition. Upper Saddle River, NJ: Prentice Hall.

Peterson, Paul E. 1981. *City Limits*. Chicago: University of Chicago Press.

Phillips, E. Barbara. 2010. *City Lights Urban-Suburban Life in the Global Society*, 3rd edition. New York: Oxford University Press.

Podover, Saul K. (Revised by Jacob W. Landynski). 1995. *The Living U.S. Constitution*, 3rd revised edition. New York: The Penguin Group.

Press, Charles and Kenneth VerBurg. 1983. *State and Community Governments in the Federal System*, 2nd edition. New York: John Wiley & Sons.

Saltzstein, Alan L. and Colin Copus, Raphael J. Sonenshein, and Chris Steckler. 2008. "Visions of Urban Reform Comparing English and U.S. Strategies for Improving City Government." *Urban Affairs Review*, Volume 44, Number 2. pp. 155–181.

Waste, Robert J. 1998. *Independent Cities Rethinking U.S. Urban Policy*._New York: Oxford University Press.

Wilson, James Q. and John J. DiIulio. 1998. *American Government*, 7th ed. Boston: Houghton Mifflin.

CHAPTER 2
Citizenship in the Federal System

1. Among the total of 83,000 local governments in the United States, identify several of the local governments in the area in which you live. Describe ways in which these compete and cooperate with one another.

2. Describe some of the ways your local government might be different if the United States were a unitary nation? What do you regard as advantages or disadvantages of this unitary system, in contrast to the existing federal system?

3. Describe an example of how the "Commerce Clause" is used by the federal government to limit the authority of the policies of a local government.

4. Make a list of twelve different laws (ordinances) which you must obey on a daily basis. Then, go back and decide whether each one originates from the federal government, your state government, or your local government. In the space provided, describe which of the three levels of government is responsible for each of the laws in your survey. According to your survey, most of the laws that affect you originate from which level of government?

5. Citizenship implies a whole series of rights as well as responsibilities to all the levels of governments under which you live. Describe which level you feel you owe the greatest amount of your responsibilities? Why? Which level is the most protective of your rights? Why?

CHAPTER 3

THE CITY MAINTAINS ITSELF - PUBLIC WORKS

—Claire L. Felbinger

Building cities is exciting, fun, and personally edifying. Those who design and construct them have permanent monuments of their contribution to the built environment. Others take credit for proposing and financing these accomplishments at ground breakings and again at ribbon cutting ceremonies. Still others have their legacy honored by having their names associated with buildings or landmarks—either by virtue of their dedicated public service or by purchasing the "naming rights" to a facility.

However, there is no ground breaking ceremony when a city worker patches a pothole, and there are no ribbons cut when water mains are lined to prevent leaking and infiltration. The day-to-day work of thousands of city workers involves operating and maintaining these structures over time. *The city maintains itself* primarily through actions associated with the Public Works profession. This chapter will define Public Works and its functions, operationalize city maintenance functions, and discuss the general nature of urban service delivery.

WHAT ARE PUBLIC WORKS?

More than two hundred years ago, Adam Smith wrote that the functions of government should be limited to providing for the national defense, affording the protection of law, and *undertaking indispensable public works*. The International City/County Management Association has offered a definition adapted from the founder of the American Public Works Association, Donald C. Stone:

> PUBLIC WORKS ARE THE PHYSICAL STRUCTURES AND FACILITIES THAT ARE DEVELOPED OR ACQUIRED BY PUBLIC AGENCIES TO HOUSE GOVERNMENTAL FUNCTIONS AND PROVIDE WATER, POWER, WASTE DISPOSAL, TRANSPORTATION, AND SIMILAR SERVICES, AND ARE MANAGED BY EXPERIENCED, INTELLIGENT, DEDICATED PROFESSIONALS TO FACILITATE AND ENSURE CONTINUOUSLY BETTER SERVICE TO THE PUBLIC. (STONE 1974: 2–3).

These "indispensable" public works are the systems and facilities which ensure the health, safety, and convenience of citizens. Oftentimes, they are referred to as urban **infrastructure** systems although the term is a little limiting. Although public works professionals are involved in the building of the public city, the majority of their work is spent in operating, maintaining, and improving the quality of these systems. The American Public Works Association (APWA) has identified 145 different functions that are related to public works (APWA, 1990) and classifies them as municipal engineering, equipment services, transportation, water resources, solid wastes, building and grounds, administrative management, and special services. Some examples of these functions are in Table 3.1. An easy way to think about public works functions is that everything a city does outside of city hall which is not police and fire related is probably a public works function.

The people who perform public works functions are as varied as the number of those functions. Civil engineers are involved in the design, construction, and maintenance decisions of urban public works services. Laborers and skilled crafters perform functions from picking up residential solid wastes to installing

TABLE 3.1 | *Public Works Functions*

Streets and highways	Engineering
Street cleaning	Solid-waste collections
Snow removal	Solid-waste disposal
Street lighting	Solid-waste billing
Street striping (marking)	Building inspection
Street signs	Building maintenance
Surveying	Custodial services
Traffic engineering	Construction inspection
Traffic signals	Park maintenance
Traffic signs	Cemetery operation
Water treatment	Radio system
Water distribution	Parking meter system
Water meter reading	Equipment maintenance
Water utility billing	Animal control
Water service	Computer operation
Sewage treatment	Electric power distribution
Sewage collection system	Electric power billing
Sewer utility billing	Gas power distribution
Storm sewer system	Gas billing
Storm water management	Street tree planting and maintenance
Zoning/subdivision control	Airport services

Source: Felbinger, C. L. (1994). Public Works. In J. M. Banovetz, D. A. Dolan, & J. W. Swain (Eds.), Managing Small Cities and Towns: A Practical Guide, p. 105

telecommunication equipment. Chemists and other technicians test the quality of a city's drinking water and the treated sewage which is reintroduced into rivers and lakes. Public administrators develop plans to finance and manage these vital services. Planners oversee the ordered linking of physical systems. These are only examples of the variety of people involved in the daily delivery of public works services. For an idea on how public works agencies are organized see Exhibit 3.1.

ISSUES OF INFRASTRUCTURE AND MAINTENANCE

Unfortunately, most people do not pay attention to public works services until they stop working. The services are taken for granted. When they turn on the tap expecting water to come out, they probably never stop to think about its purity, they merely assume it. When they flush the toilet, all of their responsibility for that waste goes away. Those who have encountered breaks in critical public works services understand how inconvenient that is. However, public works routinely work and they continue to work through systematic routine maintenance.

Deferred maintenance of public works systems was considered the prime suspect for, what was termed in the 1980s, our "crumbling urban infrastructure." Pat Choate and Susan Walter (1983) raised public consciousness of this in their book, *America in Ruins.* As a result, in 1984 Congress established the National Council on Public Works Improvement whose mission was to prepare a report on the state of the Nation's infrastructure. Over five thousand pages of research material were prepared over a two-year period contributing to the Council's 1988 final report: *Fragile Foundations.* The graphic presentation in the report which caught the eyes of Congress and the Nation was a Report Card scoring eight public works services with grades which varied from a "B" (for water resources) to a "D" (for hazardous waste). The Council proclaimed the Nation's overall infrastructure grade to be a "C"—barely passing. Once again, the main contributor to this condition is deferred maintenance. Periodic updates to the initial Report Card document only minor improvements at the aggregate or national level.

EXHIBIT 3.1

Organization of Public Works

There is no standard or recommended organizational structure for fulfilling local government public works functions. There is not even agreement about what should be included under the label public works. Some communities, for example, place functions such as code enforcement, traffic engineering, and parkway maintenance under public works; others place such functions elsewhere (e.g., code enforcement in a building department, traffic engineering in the police department; and parkway maintenance in the parks department). Some communities place all vehicle maintenance in the public works department. Others give each operating department the responsibility for maintaining its own vehicles, or they contract out this service.

Some communities place all public works functions in a single department; others place responsibility for streets and sidewalks in a public works department but have a separate water department; sanitation department (to remove and dispose of solid waste, wastewater, or both); building and grounds department; forestry department (for street trees); and engineering department. There is no evidence to suggest that one or another organizational pattern is better; size of community, range of public works function, complexity of operations, and idiosyncratic local considerations all combine to shape the organization's structures.

The appointment of a person with a background in civil engineering as director of public works has been common practice for many years. More recently this practice has begun to give way to the employment of public works directors who have training and experience in public administration. Some communities now require their public works director to have a master of public administration (MPA) degree and work experience in a public works department. The need to use the services of consultants with highly specialized engineering knowledge and the increasing complexity of government management suggest that administrative training and experience will be increasingly demanded of public works directors in the future.

Source: Felbinger, C.L. (1994). Public Works. In J.M. Banovetz, D.A. Dolan, & J.W. Swain (Eds.) Managing Small Cities and Towns: A Practical Guide, p.104

If North Americans are so good at building the public city, why have we been so bad at maintaining it? Four contributors are: the influence of federal infrastructure policy, the hidden nature of infrastructure, the balance of financial tradeoffs at the local level, and the lack of political payoff for maintenance activities.

Federally Influenced Deferred Maintenance

Until recently, the federal government funded only the construction of new infrastructure systems or the replacement of those which had exhausted their usable life. Routine maintenance was considered both a fiscal and operational responsibility of local governments. One unintended consequence of this is that some public works managers allowed infrastructure systems to deteriorate to such a condition that they would be eligible for federal government replacement grants rather than extending the life of the systems through locally funded annual maintenance. Although this saved the citizens of those communities short-term maintenance expenditures, the ultimate impact is that all citizens bear the burden of higher cost replacement of structures with shorter usable lives. The cumulative impact of such decisions is that taxpayers are paying a higher cost to maintain the integrity of infrastructure systems. An example of this is illustrated in Exhibit 3.2.

Deferral of Maintenance of "Hidden" Systems

The second reason for deferred maintenance is that many infrastructure systems are simply hidden from view. Many are underground, such as water and wastewater systems, while some are even underwater, like bridge foundations. The prevailing attitude had been that if one is receiving the service (e.g., drinking water, sewage flow, access across a river), then the infrastructure must be adequate. Clearly, this is not always the case.

For example, New York City once had a policy of "maintaining" water mains by replacing ones which either collapsed by structural failure or exploded under the pressure of the gravity fed system. As long as the pipes were hidden and people were getting water, the system was considered in good condition. However, these old mains were insulated with asbestos packing. When they exploded, asbestos dust was spewn into the air, causing even more health risks for citizens and potentially debilitating liability for the city.

It has been only recently that new technologies such as remote control video machines, leak detection devices, and nondestructive testing of structures have been used to assist in inspecting these systems. Civil engineering research is working to improve these technologies for the public works profession.

Balancing Financial Tradeoffs

A third rationale for deferred maintenance is that during times of fiscal austerity, it may seem easier for a local politician to put off scheduled maintenance and use that money for other popular services (particularly ones that people can see). Once an administration gets into the habit of deferring maintenance to the future (and, maybe future administrations), it is taking a chance that the structures may fail. In essence, they are betting that threats to health, safety, and convenience will not occur during their term in office.

EXHIBIT 3.2

Impact of a Federal Policy

An example of federally influenced deferred maintenance is provided by federal policy regarding the use of the federal Airport and Airway Trust Fund. The federal government will not finance maintenance through the fund, but it will replace runways that are beyond repair. Rather than spending local money to extend the life of runways, local officials are prompted to close them down (an inconvenience to citizens) and construct new runways on the same site, using federal dollars.

Source: Felbinger, C.L. (1994). Public Works. In J.M. Banovetz, D.A. Dolan, & J.W. Swain (Eds.), Managing Small Cities and Towns: A Practical Guide, p.107

Of course, sometimes they lose those bets—with disastrous results. Three well-known examples include the collapse of the Mianus River Bridge near Greenwich, Connecticut, in 1983; the destruction of the Cypress Viaduct of the Nimitz Freeway during the 1989 earthquake; the Great Chicago Flood in 1992 caused by an accident exacerbating the deferred maintenance of underground tunnels. These examples indicate how rolling the dice on maintenance can potentially cost millions of dollars and many lives.

Lack of Political Payoff

Another reason advanced for the deferral of maintenance was implied at the beginning of this chapter—there does not seem to be any payoff for politicians to embrace maintenance. Politicians and other professional administrators like to be associated with activities which indicate that growth and development is occurring in the city. New programs and new structures are celebrated with events such as ground breakings and ribbon cuttings. Routine maintenance is just that—routine—and is seen as rather dull and mundane by "political" standards.

All four of these reasons advanced for the decision to defer maintenance should be seen as reinforcing each other, thereby increasing the odds that maintenance will take a back seat to other local expenditures. Even enlightened public officials may not understand the importance of maintenance, since it can be complicated or made confusing by technically trained people who cannot communicate with officials and other citizens in a way they can understand. Fortunately, the *Fragile Foundations* report raised the consciousness of the nation to the plight of our crumbling urban infrastructure. It is the job of the public works profession to keep maintenance a high priority with public officials.

MAINTENANCE STRATEGIES

Public works professionals organize their infrastructure maintenance strategies around the three R's: **repair**, **rehabilitation**, and **replacement**. Repair and rehabilitation extend the life of infrastructure systems and are usually funded by local government operating budgets. City employees from the Public Works Department often perform the work. Repair involves correcting a minor problem such as filling a pothole or patching a roof. Repair maintains the integrity of existing structures—in this case, a roadway and a building. Rehabilitation is a process by which the quality of an existing structure is improved or the structure is restored to its original condition. Rehabilitation usually means the structure is strengthened or major members are replaced. If pothole patching is repair, then an asphalt overlay on a street would be considered rehabilitation.

Replacement involves the demolition of an existing structure or facility and the construction of a new and improved one. Replacement is typically funded out of a city's capital (not operating) budget. Large scale replacement projects (like the building of a new City Hall or a four-lane commuting bridge) often outstrip the city's workforce capacity, resulting in the contracting out of various aspects of the system's replacement. (Contracting will be covered later in this chapter.)

Since one cannot infinitely extend the life of an infrastructure system, replacement is, indeed, part of the city's capital improvement program. An integrated maintenance strategy includes ongoing repair and rehabilitation and plans for eventual replacement of systems. The goal is to efficiently prolong the life of the infrastructure, which ultimately saves tax dollars.

MAINTAINING HUMAN INFRASTRUCTURE

If maintenance of urban infrastructure takes a back seat to other types of funding, the maintenance of its human infrastructure system is even more rarely addressed. When we speak about maintaining human infrastructure, we are referring to training and equipping those who manage, maintain, and direct the operations of infrastructure systems with the tools to most effectively do their jobs. Unfortunately, those activities most closely associated with human infrastructure improvement—attendance at training and workshop events, adoption of technological innovations, research and development—are often the first items cut in budgets during times of fiscal austerity.

The vast majority of respondents to an American Public Works Association survey indicated that a formal management degree or at least course offerings in continuing education in management (in addition to an engineering degree) are important ingredients to successful management of public works agencies in the twenty-first century. This continuing maintenance is not limited to the top management. Middle managers and supervisors often take advantage of workshops targeted to them from their professional associations such as the APWA, the Water Environment Federation, the American Water Works Association, and their affiliated state chapters.

Investments in human infrastructure also come in the form of support for research in civil engineering related materials and processes and the technology transfer activities associated with those who relate basic civil engineering research to actual practice. The ring of people involved in this enterprise is much wider than that typically considered in maintenance of our physical infrastructure and even includes those involved in management research and planning.

DELIVERING LOCAL SERVICES EFFECTIVELY

Historically, the largest portions of a city's budget have gone to public works and public safety functions—those services provided outside of City Hall. Therefore, it is appropriate in a chapter on public works to discuss the nature of public services, the alternate arrangements for the delivery of those services, and the administrative issues which must be balanced regarding decisions about how urban services are delivered.

Despite the Adam Smith quote at the beginning of this chapter, we all know that cities currently are involved in more than what could be considered traditional public works and public safety services. Today, cities provide services which at one time might have been the purview of one's family, church, or charitable organization. These include social services, recreation, health care, daycare, cultural institutions and events, and many other non-traditional services. This illustrates the very nature of city services—they are not static. They evolve as cities develop and change to meet the emerging needs of citizens.

If the notion of what services a city should provide changes over time, it is reasonable that the idea of who should be in the best position to deliver services can also come into question. The answer is seldom clear cut. It can be a function of local tradition, union contracts, or even the personality of an administrator. During the 1980s, privatization of public service delivery was considered the most efficient delivery method. In the 1990s the reinventing and re-engineering experts favored having "entrepreneurial governments" arrange for service delivery. Now, the decisions on service delivery arrangements are not as clear cut. The decisions are more complex and require considerations of all delivery procedures based on the service, the history of the city, and the qualifications of the municipal labor force. Urban scholars have argued that it is the *nature* of goods and services which suggests appropriate methods of service delivery. The following sections discuss the nature of goods and services, alternate methods of service delivery (who will be involved), and managing local service delivery (how the service will be delivered).

IDENTIFYING THE NATURE OF GOODS AND SERVICES

The previous section demonstrated that service responsibility can shift over time—for example, what had been the responsibility of the family could shift to a city responsibility. Regardless, is there something constant about the basic nature of services which will assist in identifying the most logical service delivery mechanism? Most urban researchers have agreed that all services can be categorized on two continua based on their qualities of exclusion and consumption. This typology was developed by Vincent and Elinor Ostrom (1977) and further refined by E. S. Savas (1982).

A good or service is characterized as **exclusive** if a supplier can exclude someone from its access until conditions of the supplier are met. It is easy to understand exclusion if one thinks about any store purchase. The owner of the store can prohibit a customer from consuming a good until the price (the condition of sale set by the owner) is paid. If the customer chooses to try to consume the good without paying (stealing), the owner can prosecute. The continuum of exclusivity is based on how feasible it is to exclude someone from the good or service.

The characteristic of **consumption** deals with whether more than one person can use or consume the good without diminishing the quality to another person. Jointly consumed goods can be enjoyed equally by any number of individuals while individually consumed goods' qualities are denied to others by virtue of their consumption. The classic example of joint consumption involves the "consumption" of a network program on television. The "quality" of the program remains unchanged whether one or one hundred thousand people view the program. The addition of one additional viewer does not alter the quality for any of the other viewers. In the same way, when a viewer turns off the program, the quality afforded to the other viewers is neither reduced nor enhanced. On the other hand, when one "consumes" or buys a television, others are denied access to that particular television; the use of *that* television is denied to others.

The concepts of exclusion and consumption are used to define the ideal types of services a city can provide. (The definition of the term "ideal type" is the sociological one—a pure type—and not one "ideally suited" to local delivery.) **Private goods** are those which are individually consumed and for which exclusion is entirely feasible. Given the earlier "exclusion" discussions, these are functions or services which could easily be provided by market systems. In other words, the market can operate in such a way that it could extract a fee from a citizen to provide a service and exclude the citizen if payment were not made. The best examples of private urban services are solid waste collection and recreational services. In solid waste collection citizens can be charged for the pickup of wastes either by volume (number of bags) or routine (once a week) and a bill could be given to residents. In the case of recreation activities, a department could charge user fees (which may be publicly subsidized) which would allow someone to participate in their activities. If one did not pay, that citizen could be denied access to the activity. These are the sorts of activities which could be **contracted** out to firms rather than be the sole responsibility of existing departments. In other words, private goods, by their nature, are more amenable to being contracted out than other urban services since their qualities of being individually consumed and the ease with which someone can be excluded from the service fit best with provision by a private vendor—their operations are most nearly like those operative in the private market system.

Another ideal type includes services for which exclusion is feasible and for which consumption is of a joint nature. These services are called **toll goods**. The provision of cable television services, in contrast to network service, is a good example. Like network service, cable television program quality is neither enhanced nor decreased based on the number of viewers at any particular time. However, access *to the programming is limited to those who pay for the installation of the cable system and the monthly service fee.*

Another example of a toll good is a toll road. Operation of a toll road works best on limited access highways (exclusion is feasible) where agencies can extract a charge or toll for using the roadway. Presumably, motorists would be willing to pay for the convenience of driving on a higher speed roadway which had fewer turns and no traffic signals in order to reach their destination more quickly. While government typically provides a route by which any driver could reach a destination free of charge, operators of toll roads extract a convenience fee from those who wish to bypass small towns or travel on a higher speed roadway. Currently tolls are proposed on existing free highways to alleviate congestion. Variable rate tolls allow drivers the choice to bypass free lanes which might be congested. The tolls can vary by time of day and amount of congestion. Oftentimes special district governments operate these facilities; however, it is not inconceivable that other market driven private parties may provide such transportation alternatives. In both cases, the fees extracted from the tolls are used to repair, rehabilitate, and ultimately replace the roadway. Therefore, the tolls should reflect the actual cost of these activities.

The third ideal type consists of **common pool goods**. In this case, the goods are individually consumed; however, exclusion is impossible. When exclusion is impossible, then extracting a fee for service is infeasible. Rational economic actors will use up the good or service since it is essentially free. The problem for society is that this creates a situation in which the good or service can be exhausted or destroyed in the process.

The classic examples of common pool goods are natural resources. The breathable air, fish in lakes, and the beauty of wilderness areas all can be jointly consumed or enjoyed. It is infeasible to charge individuals for their enjoyment of these resources. It would simply cost too much to staff the fee collection system. Moreover, many believe that access to these resources is a right of citizenship and should not bear a cost. However, there is a role for government with respect to these services and that is regulation. Automobile emission standards and their associated penalties act to ensure the air quality. Limitations on the size and number of fish which can be caught in an area are enforced by rangers in order to safeguard the resource for future generations. Restrictions on the number of visitors in national parks or restrictions on areas they may visit regulate the use and over use of those areas. Again, a proper role for the government in the provision of common pool goods is to ensure their continued access through regulation.

The fourth and final ideal type of goods and services is that for which the consumption is joint and for which exclusion is infeasible. These are called **collective goods**. The market seldom becomes involved in the delivery of collective goods since there is no incentive to do so—one cannot exact a fee and "free riders" will use the good without paying. While some argue that collective goods cause the most problems for society (presumably since the market seldom gets involved), the more lucid argument is that it is in the delivery of collective goods that governments should be involved. In fact, they are the best, and sometimes only, reasonable providers of collective services.

National defense is the best example of a collective good provided by the government. All citizens of the United States, as well as any legal or illegal aliens residing in the country, receive the same level of national defense. Whether one agrees with defense policy or not, the government does not differentiate among its citizens with regard to defense. Moreover, it could not differentiate, since exclusion is infeasible. One cannot opt out of national defense since the consumption is joint. A pacifist receives the same level of national defense as a militarist whether they like it or not. National defense policy is justifiably debated and formed through the workings of government and collectively provided to all citizens and non-citizens alike.

At the local level, emergency preparedness and security are examples of a collective good in the public works arena. Expenditures for preparedness benefit everyone living in or driving through a city regardless if one happens to be in a flood plain, along a railroad, downtown, or in any residential area. The same amount and quality of security accrues to all in the community. It would be physically and politically infeasible for local governments to exclude citizens from this protection.

Unfortunately, not all urban services fit neatly into the four ideal type categories outlined here. As mentioned before, they may shift to and from ideal types based on society's determination regarding individual rights and the role of government in ensuring these rights. One problem with the push to privatize all services in the name of efficiency and effectiveness of private markets was the absence of an understanding of the underlying nature of goods and services which identifies appropriate roles for various sectors in providing different types of services. Having this understanding, urban service managers can propose alternate modes of service delivery in a more informed manner.

ALTERNATE METHODS OF SERVICE DELIVERY

E. S. Savas (1987) provides a useful distinction about various city officials' roles in the delivery of urban services: **arrangers, producers**, and **consumers**. Arrangers organize and ensure the service is delivered, producers directly supply the service, while consumers ultimately receive or use the service. Sometimes these roles are blurred; however, just as the ideal types described earlier, a focus on these roles allows easier understanding of the alternate modes of urban service delivery.

Table 3.2 displays a range of service delivery modes which range from total government involvement to no governmental involvement. None of these modes is "best," rather, in certain situations, one may be more appropriate than another based on the nature of the good or service involved.

The traditional method of urban service delivery is **governmental service**. In this mode, the government acts as both the arranger and producer of local services which are consumed by its citizens. Local policy dictates the level and frequency of service while governmental employees directly deliver the service. A city's policy to pick up residential solid waste once a week, every week, using city employees and city refuse packing trucks is an example of governmental service.

When a city arranges for another unit of government to deliver services to its citizens, it is involved in an **intergovernmental agreement**. Typically, a larger unit of government provides the service for another smaller unit of government taking advantage of economies of scale. For example, many cities in Los Angeles County use the paramedic services of the county government. In these cases, each city arranges with the county to directly provide services to its citizens. The county then negotiates a fee for service with the city, the costs of which are either borne by the city (through the general fund) or shared by the city and the citizen-user of the service. In rapidly growing areas in which a private market does not exist, a new city may ask an adjoining city to collect its residential solid waste for a fee if the city is not in a position to purchase packing trucks or hire sanitation employees.

The method of service delivery most closely associated with the term "privatization" in North America is **contracting** out service delivery to a private sector firm. Given the nature of goods and services, it seems reasonable that contracting out works best with services which approximate private or toll goods. In those services, the private market has some incentive to be involved in the delivery of the service. In contracting out, the government arranges for a private (or sometimes non-profit) sector firm to deliver a specified quantity and quality of service to its citizens. Note that in contracting that the government does not relinquish all involvement with the service. It provides policy direction, oversight, and evaluation of service quality—the arrangement function— while the firm produces the service. Where contracts have supplied poor services to citizens, it is usually the fault of the government for not assuming its oversight authority and often not having performance standards specifically written in the contract. In the case of solid waste collection, a city can contract with a private firm to provide residential collection once a week, every week with a minimum of missed pickups and spills. The firm would use its own trucks and employees and would be responsible for responding to citizen complaints.

TABLE 3.2 | *Alternate Service Delivery Arrangements*

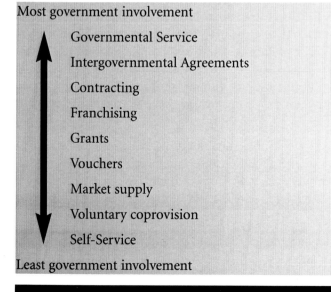

Most government involvement
- Governmental Service
- Intergovernmental Agreements
- Contracting
- Franchising
- Grants
- Vouchers
- Market supply
- Voluntary coprovision
- Self-Service

Least government involvement

While contracting out works best with goods which approximate private or toll goods, it is also most useful for services which can be classified either as mundane and repetitive, or highly technical. Collection of solid wastes is one example of a repetitive task; data entry, road striping, and tree trimming are others. In terms of technical skills, smaller cities often contract out for engineering services, since it would be too expensive relative to the workload to have a full-time engineer on staff. Larger cities with engineering departments will often contract out large engineering projects to private design and engineering firms as the workload exceeds their capacity. In these cases, the engineering department maintains an oversight role over the conduct of the contracted engineering services.

Franchising involves the awarding of monopoly privileges to a firm to provide a service. In a franchising arrangement, the government arranges for the service but usually with strict regulation of fees and the imposition of performance standards. Most cable television and other utility operations are performed under franchise agreements, since it is infeasible for a provider of this kind of service to compete door to door for service provision due to the high capital and startup costs associated with these types of services.

Sometimes governments offer subsidies to private vendors or other authorities to provide a needed service which would not necessarily be a profitable undertaking. These subsidies are called **grants**. The most common local examples are mass transit and housing. In the case of mass transit, the local government perceives a need for low cost transportation for all its citizens and arranges and entices (with the grant subsidy) the involvement of a contractor to provide the service. In housing, grants are often used to encourage developers to include units designated for low to moderate income citizens.

Vouchers, on the other hand, involve providing subsidies directly to the consumer, allowing them the free choice of service vendors and relatively free choice of products. The government broadly arranges the service and the consumers have the choice of vendors. The easiest example to understand is the Food Stamp program. Citizens are given stamps (vouchers) which they can use to purchase items (the variety of which is regulated by the government) at the grocery store of their choice. Once at the store, they can choose the brands or cuts of food they wish. Housing vouchers function the same way. The vendors (grocery stores, landlords) then redeem the vouchers from the government for cash.

Use of **market** structures (the private sector) to deliver local services works best when the goods and services approach private or toll types, when there is a need for a service, and when there are multiple vendors who wish to produce the product. This is also the best time for government to get out of the business of providing a service directly since the market forces will ensure that the service is delivered at a competitive price. Strategically, this is the best opportunity for local governments to "load shed" costly services.

When citizen-consumers get involved directly in the provision of a good or service, they are participating in what is referred to as **coprovision or coproduction** of services. One type of coprovision is the use of volunteer groups to augment city services. For example, a Garden Club can volunteer to beautify the grounds around City Hall or provide plants to decorate a traffic circle. Increasingly, people and groups volunteer to keep a portion of highways free of litter—Adopt a Highway programs. These voluntary efforts do not necessarily take the place of city services. For example, if a citizen fails to pick up litter on the highway, the unit of government responsible will get the phone call to clean up the mess. Voluntary service provision works best when it enhances existing city services. Its global utilization for delivering local services was overstated in many policy speeches of the 1980s.

Self-Service is a method in which citizens take responsibility for most, if not all, aspects of service delivery and usually takes one of two forms. In the first form, the government relinquishes responsibility for a service forcing citizens to arrange and provide the service. For example, if a city gets out of the business of arranging for residential solid waste collection, citizens would have to arrange and pay for a vendor to pick up their refuse or transport it themselves to a landfill.

The second form of self-service is to take private actions to reduce the need for public services. For example, using a kitchen sink garbage disposal reduces the need for solid waste collection services by reducing the volume of waste (although it increases the need for wastewater treatment). Locking the doors to one's house or car or installing alarm devices reduces the need for police services by discouraging thieves in the first place.

Any comprehensive approach to organizing the delivery of local services should take into account the nature of the goods and services involved, the variety of delivery methods available, and the needs and convenience of citizens. In some cases, citizens are willing to pay for high quality services produced by governmental employees while others would rather see the service contracted out or even dropped. There is not one good answer for every city. However, considering the nature and variety of delivery mechanisms is a good strategy for effectively providing urban services.

MANAGING LOCAL SERVICES

Examining the nature of locally delivered services and considering the range of delivery alternatives deals only with the input portion of the services. It does not estimate the impact of those deliberations on citizens. Every decision about the management of local services has both intended and unintended impacts on citizens. This section introduces some of the concepts which must be balanced in any service delivery operation.

Equality versus Equity

The concept of equality in service delivery is deceptively easy for most managers, politicians, and citizens to understand. Most would agree that services should be delivered "equally" to all citizens without regard to race, class, or power stature. However, equality is often operationalized in practice as providing equal *inputs* of service in each geographical area. City council members want equal dollars expended on each service in each ward. Equal numbers of crews should be deployed in each route. Equal numbers of squad cars should patrol each district.

While this concept of equality would be considered "fair" to all parties, it does not take into account differential needs of geographically dispersed citizens. Some neighborhoods are more densely populated, older, or have different crime rates. If one is concerned with the equality of *output* after a service has been delivered, (e.g., same condition of cleanliness of neighborhoods or similar crime rates), then *unequal inputs* may be necessary. More squad cars should be deployed, more crews dispatched, or different machinery used. The equality of the result of service is referred to as **equity**. Unfortunately, it is more difficult to measure outputs than inputs. An unintended consequence of a policy of providing equal inputs can be an inequitable service outcome—unequal service conditions. It is the job of the manager of local services to measure service outputs and convince elected officials of the need to concentrate on citizens' conditions after the service is delivered ("safe streets," "decent, safe, and sanitary housing") rather than focus on the more easily measured inputs (dollars and crews).

Efficiency versus Effectiveness

As a concept, efficiency refers to getting the most service per dollar of input. The efficiency of the private sector was often cited as the dominant rationale for contracting out urban services in the 1980s. Effectiveness concerns doing the right things correctly. Of course, effectiveness also involves performing services within budget and as efficiently as possible. However, often elected officials and managers focus so much on efficiency that they do not bother to ask questions like, "Should we really be doing this?" or "Is there something else we should be doing for citizens?" Developing service-based missions, operationalizing outcomes, and evaluating success toward achieving performance standards are the steps by which good urban managers and elected officials balance the concepts of efficiency versus effectiveness.

Ethics

Ethics takes on a major role in the delivery of urban services. Sometimes the qualities which one would value in the private sector (e.g., profit, power, privacy) are not reasonable in the public sector. In the public sector things not only have to *be* good, they have to *look* good to citizens. Managers of public sector services in urban areas are held to a much higher standard than their private sector counterparts and the unintended consequences of behavior are subject to more scrutiny. *The city maintains itself* as it maintains the integrity of its infrastructure—both physical and human—its political systems, and its ethical standards.

CHAPTER 3
The City Maintains Itself - Public Works

1. Observe the route you take from your home to this class and answer the following questions:
    - How many bridges did you cross? _____
    - How many vacant buildings did you pass? _____
    - How many parks did you see? _____
    - How many new commercial construction sites were in progress? _____
    - How many fast food outlets were there? _____
    - How many schools were there? _____
    - Sketch the route, showing the landscape features mentioned above.

2. Give specific examples of exclusive goods and consumption goods in your central city:

3. In the urban delivery system, give an example of:

an arranger

a producer

a consumer

CHAPTER **4**

THE SKELETON OF POWER

—Barbara Phillips

"WHO RUNS THIS TOWN?"

That sounds like a simple question, but it's deceptive. And as with most questions worth asking, serious observers answer in different ways.

Political scientists, lawyers, and public administrators often approach this question by examining a city's legal structure. This is because, as President Franklin D. Roosevelt once said, "structure is government." Knowing what cities and city officials can do legally is vital to understanding who runs any town.

But a city's legal structure reveals only a small part of the story. Local politics now takes place within a larger, often global, context of public and private institutions.

In the United States, knowing how a city fits into the web of intergovernmental and corporate relations—spinning out from, say, Beijing or other international capitals to Washington, D.C., sometimes bypassing the state capital, and weaving its way down to city hall—is important for understanding who and what run U.S. towns. But understanding the networks of informal power and influence may be more important, perhaps crucial, in figuring out who has the ability to get things done. For instance, Chicago's city charter contains no mention of party bosses or ethnic voting blocs. Nor does it refer to the influence of global corporations, Internet-based businesses (e.g., eBay, gambling sites), "body shops" (government contractors, such as the very profitable Science Applications International Corporation [SAIC], a San Diego-based private corporation with 44,000 employees—more than the U.S. Departments of Labor, Energy, and Housing and Urban Development combined), nationwide religious groups, organized crime, street gangs, and other interest groups on public policy. Yet these individuals and organizations can be key actors in city politics. Thus, both formal and informal power structures—at both the micro and macro levels—need to be examined before any conclusions are reached about who runs any town.

City Lights: Urban-Suburban Life in the Global Society, 3rd Edition by Phillips (2009) Chp. 13 "The Skeleton of Power" pp. 423–463 © author. By permission of Oxford University Press, Inc.

This chapter looks at the public institutional frame work of local government in the United States—only. Why *only* the United States? Because globally local governments differ so widely that justice cannot be done to their range in one chapter. Further, the organization of local government can be dizzyingly confusing. Even to the locals! Take towns in Great Britain, for example. One British guidebook notes, "The set-up of UK Local Government is extremely confusing even to those of us who live here" (Edkins, n.d.).

This chapter investigates questions such as these: How are U.S. cities legally organized? What power and formal authority do city officials have? How do cities interact with other units of government in the U.S. federal system?

First, a word about the name of the game: power. Like love, truth, beauty, and other abstract concepts, power can be defined in at least 100 ways. Here, *power* means the ability to force an individual or group to do something, even if they resist.

Ultimately, power is rooted in the threat of force or its actual use. People in many cities across the globe, from Port-au-Prince, Haiti, to Kigali, Rwanda, and Monrovia, Liberia, to New York City, Madrid, Najaf, and Kabul understand that the accepted balance of power can be upset by anyone brandishing a lethal weapon. Even a 10-year-old with a gun, stones, brick, or machete can become powerful.

Power can be distinguished from authority and influence. By **authority**, we mean legitimate power, power used in such a way that people see it as legitimate. By *influence*, we mean informal power, sometimes based on persuasion. Chicago gangster Al Capone, both powerful and influential (but lacking in authority), understood the difference: He once said, "You can get much farther with a kind word and a gun than you can with a kind word alone (in http://www.quotemountain.com/famous_quote_author/al_capone_famous_quotations/)."

We begin with an overview of governmental power and authority. In particular, we examine the role that citizens think government should play in their lives.

THE SCOPE OF GOVERNMENT

"That government which governs least governs best." Jefferson's saying reflects the deep distrust many people in the United States feel toward government at any level, no matter who runs it. Fear of excessive government and centralized, faraway authority is a recurrent theme in U.S. history, rooted in the Jeffersonian ideals of liberty and small government.

Government's Limited Scope in the United States

For ideological reasons, the scope of government in the United States is smaller and weaker than that of any other major country in the world today. In France, England, and Sweden, for instance, government is expected to regulate the extent and nature of physical growth and to oversee the general health and welfare of its citizenry. And, as Table 4.1 shows, many countries collect much more revenue per capita to pay for such services. But the dominant ideology in the United States assigns as much responsibility as possible to the private, rather than the public, sector.

TABLE 4.1 | *Gross Domestic Product (GDP), Tax Revenues, and Population for Selected Countries, 2003*

	Gross Domestic Product, Tax Revenue & Population, 2003				
	GDP millions of US $	GDP per capita	Tax Revenue millions of US $	Tax Revenue per capita	Population thousands
Australia	527,975	$ 26,402	166,840	$ 8,343	19,998
Austria	255,146	$ 31,432	109,968	$ 13,547	8,118
Belgium	304,352	$ 29,337	138,176	$ 13,319	10,374

	Gross Domestic Product, Tax Revenue & Population, 2003				
	GDP millions of US $	GDP per capita	Tax Revenue millions of US $	Tax Revenue per capita	Population thousands
Canada	873,914	$ 27,630	295,383	$ 9,339	31,629
Czech Republic	90,488	$ 8,870	34,114	$ 3,344	10,202
Denmark	211,238	$ 39,190	102,028	$ 18,929	5,390
Finland	161,703	$ 31,020	72,443	$ 13,897	5,213
France	1,788,032	$ 28,933	776,006	$ 12,557	61,799
Germany	2,442,915	$ 29,603	867,235	$ 10,509	82,523
Greece	173,022	$ 15,720	61,769	$ 5,612	11,007
Hungary	82,158	$ 8,112	31,631	$ 3,123	10,128
Iceland	10,387	$ 35,907	4,134	$ 14,291	289
Ireland	152,098	$ 38,111	45,173	$ 11,319	3,991
Italy	1,467,747	$ 25,265	632,599	$ 10,889	58,095
Japan	4,326,747	$ 33,905	1,094,667	$ 8,578	127,613
Korea	609,221	$ 12,731	154,133	$ 3,221	47,853
Luxembourg	27,005	$ 60,012	11,153	$ 24,785	450
Mexico	640,147	$ 6,232	121,628	$ 1,184	102,726
Netherlands	512,142	$ 31,567	198,711	$ 12,248	16,224
New Zealand	81,398	$ 20,152	28,408	$ 7,033	4,039
Norway	220,664	$ 8,339	95,768	$ 20,979	4,565
Poland	209,360	$ 5,482	71,601	$ 1,875	38,187
Portugal	147,205	$ 14,100	54,613	$ 5,231	10,440
Slovak Republic	32,614	$ 6,064	10,143	$ 1,886	5,378
Spain	879,951	$ 20,948	307,103	$ 7,311	42,006
Sweden	301,385	$ 33,644	152,501	$ 17,024	8,958
Switzerland	321,881	$ 43,468	94,955	$ 12,823	7,405
Turkey	239,442	$ 3,387	78,537	$ 1,111	70,690
United Kingdom	1,795,848	$ 30,154	639,322	$ 10,735	59,555
United States	10,942,668	$ 37,594	2,801,323	$ 9,624	291,077
OECD Average		$ 25,805		$ 8,004	

Source: OECD Revenue Statistics 1965–2004. OECD, Paris, 2004. © Urban Institute, Brookings Institution, 1439

The scope of the public sector at all levels—federal, state, and local—increased dramatically in the twentieth century as the United States changed from a country of farms and small towns to a metropolitan nation. Yet, governments still operate in a climate generally hostile to them.

Particularly after a series of widely reported scandals in high places—from Watergate in the 1970s to reports in the 2000s of corruption, payoffs, cover-ups, lying to the public, and sexual no-nos, not to mention shameless lobbying—an atmosphere of public cynicism prevails. Trust in both national government and corporate America has declined in recent years. Scandals at Enron, WorldCom, and other major corporations did not help restore confidence in big business. According to a 2002 CBS poll, only one in four people in the United States thought that corporate executives were honest. Further, only 6 percent expressed high levels of confidence in major companies (Roberts, 2002).

In the United States, trust in government has been steadily eroding for decades (see NPR-Kaiser-Kennedy School Poll, 2000). This mood is captured in one reporter's comment about Congress over a generation ago, which remains apt: "The crime rate in Congress is probably higher than in downtown Detroit (Newfield in Bogart, 1980:5r)."

For decades, conservative and libertarian groups have attacked big government and big spending. (Although the rhetoric of so-called conservatives at the national level did not match their actions, such as government bailouts of struggling financial institutions.)

At the local-state level, California's Proposition 13 (the Jarvis–Gann initiative), passed in 1978, is often named as the harbinger of a nationwide revolt against "tax-and-spend" government. This initiative amended the state's constitution in a way that reduced county property taxes, by nearly one-half, and restricted their future growth. Since many local government services are funded by the property tax, Proposition 13 effectively limited the expansion of local government service.

Why did the tax revolt happen first in California? Analysts point to one specific demographic reason– suburban growth (which provided a base for an expanding conservatism)—plus the state's involvement in trade with Asia's industrial–technological sector. Sociologist Harvey Molotch added an often overlooked factor: then skyrocketing property values. Molotch (1990:183) says that California's rising property values fueled rising property taxes: "the cutbacks blamed on Proposition 13 (including draconian budget decreases for public hospitals, paramedics, coastal protection and a proliferation of user fees for services formerly free) were due to wealth creation, rather than wealth erosion." Still, it didn't feel that way to homeowners, especially older ones on fixed incomes. On paper, their homes had increased in value. But homeowners couldn't eat or spend the profits unless they sold their homes. Thus, older homeowners, not corporate business, spearheaded Proposition 13 as a security blanket for their future.

California's cities were only the first to feel the fiscal pinch. Taxpayers' rebellions soon occurred in many states. (Joblessness played a part too: Nationwide, nearly one in seven manufacturing jobs had disappeared in the private manufacturing sector in about 3.5 years from mid-1979 to the end of 1982.)

In this economic climate, voters elected conservative political leaders. No new taxes! Reduce government spending! Privatize! These messages became rallying cries. They were the centerpiece of Margaret Thatcher's Conservative government in Great Britain (1978–1990) as well as the Reagan and George Herbert Walker Bush administrations (1980–1992).

Shortly, we will look at how federal policies affect cities. First, let's examine the impact of state policies on local government.

To begin with, starting more than a generation ago, the fiscal pinch became the fiscal crisis in many states. From the late 1970s on, downsizing was in. Due to circumstances beyond their borders (e.g., economic recession that cut into tax receipts, the credit crisis in 2007 and beyond), local governments in many states faced agonizing choices in "cutback management."

Paradoxical Attitudes Toward Government

Attitudes toward government in the United States are often paradoxical. On the one hand, voters may desire limits on government's growth. On the other, they look to government to solve many issues of collective concern. In other words, people may wish that government's powers were less, but they expect it to do more. In the case of California, some analysts of Proposition 13 concluded that what the voters wanted was something for nothing: lower taxes and more public services—simultaneously.

Public-Private Sector Relationships

Even in spheres where the U.S. government is expected to act (either as problem solver, distributor of resources and benefits, or regulator), it is assumed that public policy will be made in conjunction with private group interests.

Often, private interests play a significant, some say dominant, role in public decision making. At the local level, for example, real estate brokers and large land developers have a significant impact on zoning decisions and private business influences urban redevelopment plans. Similarly, professional organizations, unions, and corporate officials are generally consulted on policies affecting their interests. Often, such groups initiate policy proposals.

The political philosophy that underlies these public–private sector relations is rooted in classical liberalism and pluralist democracy. The dominant ideology in the United States holds that government reflects the individual citizens' wishes through group representation, and that government does not serve any one group's interest more than another's. Hence, under the theory of pluralism or interest-group democracy, government *should* act as a broker, balancing private interests.

The "Proper" Role of Local Government

The dominant U.S. ideology holds that local government should act as a forum in which competing private interests negotiate and come to an accommodation that serves the entire community's interest. In this view, government is supposed to be a facilitator of private economic activity, not an obstacle. Thus, private enterprise expects local government to set the stage for its activities by providing infrastructure (e.g., streets and sewers), maintaining police and fire protection, supporting a "good business climate" (e.g., keeping business taxes low, assuring the absence of "inappropriate" street people outside tourist hotels), and regulating certain activities to prevent chaos and quackery (e.g., land-use regulations, public-health standards).

To protect their citizens' welfare and to prevent untrammeled competition, local governments today have varying degrees of authority to intervene and regulate private business—by granting health permits to restaurants, construction permits to builders, and so forth. Clearly, the granting or withholding of such benefits can mean economic life or death to private entrepreneurs. Given these economic stakes, we could predict that local politics cannot be separated from economics. This close connection between political power and potential profit should be kept in mind when analyzing who runs any town.

To conclude: As of 2002, there were 87,525 local governments in the United States (see Table 4.2). These local governments provide a number of services and goods for collective consumption and individual betterment, ranging from well-maintained roads to legal entitlements to make money. Various groups are concerned when their interests are at stake, whether they involve getting sewer hook-ups for a suburban housing development or a neighborhood day-care center.

Local government is at the center of competing demands for its scarce resources. It can't fund all projects proposed. It can't award more than one contract to build a new school or give everyone a license to operate a taxi. And in hard economic times, such as the recessionary 2000s, it may not be able to pay both its police officers and its paramedics. In this milieu, there are bound to be conflicts of interest, opportunities for corruption, and attempts to manipulate or persuade the public via the mass media.

TABLE 4.2 | U.S. Local Governments, 1952–2002

	U.S. Government Units: 1952–2002										
Type of Government	2002	1997	1992	1987	1982	1977	1972	1967	1962	1957	1952
Total	87,900	87,504	86,743	83,237	81,831	79,913	78,269	81,299	91,236	102,392	116,805
Federal government	1	1	1	1	1	1	1	1	1	1	1
State governments	50	50	50	50	50	50	50	50	50	48	48
Local governments	87,849	87,453	86,692	83,186	81,780	79,862	78,218	81,248	91,185	102,343	116,756
General purpose	3,034	3,043	3,043	3,042	3,041	3,042	3,044	3,049	3,043	3,050	3,052
County	35,937	36,001	35,962	35,891	35,810	35,684	35,508	35,153	35,141	34,415	34,009
Municipal	19,431	19,372	19,296	19,200	19,076	18,862	18,517	18,048	17,217	16,807	
Township (school districts)	13,522	13,726	14,556	14,721	14,851	15,174	15,781	21,782	34,678	50,454	67,355
Special districts	35,356	34,683	33,131	29,532	28,078	25,962	23,885	21,264	18,323	14,424	12,340

Source: Adapted from U.S. Census Bureau, Table A, p. 5, July 2002 (http://ftp2.census.gov/govs/cog/ 2022COGprelim_report.pdf).

Local Political Environments

Local communities don't answer the normative question "What should government do?" in the same way. Some communities expect—and expect to pay for—only minimal public services. (Some communities want top-notch services, such as schools and police protection, but prefer that the services be provided by private companies.) Others demand a higher level of services and more of them. Thus, the local political environment is a key factor in analyzing the scope of local government.

According to neoconservative "public choice" theorists, people rationally choose a local political environment. For instance, when a woman chooses a particular place to live, she chooses one bundle of services over another. If she doesn't like the particular service bundle, she can vote with her car. Others disagree, saying that residential choices are due either to "forced choice," "dumb happenstance" (Molotch, 1990:195), or shared lifestyles (e.g., Weiss, 1988). Whatever their motivation for choosing one community over another, people do live in cities and suburbs that offer different services.

The following typology applies only to U.S. suburbs, classifying them according to their attitude toward economic development:

1. *Aggressive.* Suburbs that aggressively compete for business or industrial activities. Types pursuing this strategy: (1) older, close-in suburbs suffering from problems similar to those of their central city (e.g., fiscal pressure, stagnating income) and (2) newer, more prosperous suburbs.

2. *Regulatory.* Suburbs that adhere to regulations believed to be in the public interest and that are considered more important that development per se. Type pursuing this strategy: those with attractive land that can choose which development they want.

3. *Cooperative.* Suburbs that are moderately prodevelopment. Type pursuing this strategy: stable, established communities.

4. *Retentive.* Suburbs that want to retain existing businesses and industries. Type pursuing this strategy: old, stable suburbs of mixed residential-commercial activity.

5. *Reactive.* Suburbs that have no formal policy on economic development but react case by case. Type pursuing this strategy: developed suburbs (Pelissero and Fasenfest, 1988).

6. *Antidevelopment.* Suburbs that oppose economic development. Type pursuing this strategy: ecology-minded and/or upper-income suburbs.

According to the developers of this five ideal-type classification (I added the sixth type), the values of local elected officials in the suburbs they studied "shaped the particular mix of policies followed in each suburb" and "determined the suburban community's approach to development" (Pelissero and Fasenfest, 1988:11).

Whether city or suburb, the population size and mix, the values of local elected officials, and the attitudes toward economic growth influence the local political environment. So does the level of tax resources available. For instance, relatively homogeneous, residential, upper-status suburbs (e.g., PRIZM's Upper Crust) do not need to promote economic growth or mediate among conflicting interests. Large, heterogeneous cities, on the other hand, often seek to juggle conflicting interests.

CITIES AS CREATURES OF THEIR STATE

In the United States, cities are entirely creatures of their state governments. This stems from a decision made by the republic's founding fathers; they made no mention of cities in the U.S. Constitution. Instead, they granted the states the right to create or not to create all local jurisdictions, including cities.

When the states did create cities, they kept legal power over them. Hence, it is the 50 state legislatures that decide how city governments are structured.

General-Law Cities and Charter Cities

States grant legal powers to their creatures—the cities—in two different ways. Some states establish the general powers of city governments in state law; these are called general-law cities. Other states spell out the powers of a city in a charter approved by the legislature; these are called charter cities.

Charters granted to cities by their states vary in content, but most describe the form, composition, powers, and limitations of city officials. To illustrate, a city charter might state that the city council will be elected every 4 years, have one representative from each of 10 districts, and have authority over personnel, zoning, parks, and budgeting.

An important variation is the home-rule charter. Under home-rule provisions in a state constitution, the precise definition of city powers is left up to the city voters, within limits set by the state constitution. About 75 percent of large U.S. cities operate under home-rule provisions. About half of the states provide for home rule in their state constitutions, and about a dozen more allow home rule through legislation.

Charters can be revised. However, voters usually greet revision with yawns.

New York City was forced to revise its charter in 1989 after the U.S. Supreme Court ruled that the city's top government body, the Board of Estimate, was unconstitutional (because it violated the principle of one person, one vote). New Yorkers approved a complete overhaul of municipal government, eliminating the Board of Estimate, a unique legislative-executive hybrid that exercised more power than the city council.

Dillon's Rule

When a legal question arises concerning the extent of power granted by a state to a city, the courts have traditionally ruled against cities. In other words, the courts narrowly construe city powers. This narrow construction of city powers is based on Dillon's rule, named for Iowa State Judge John F. Dillon, who presided over a court decision in 1868 (see National League of Cities, n.d.).

What difference does it make if states legally control cities and if the courts narrowly interpret city powers? A great deal. Dillon's rule means that a city cannot operate a hot dog stand at the city park without first getting the state legislature to pass an enabling law, unless, by chance, the city's charter or some previously enacted law clearly covers the sale of hot dogs.

Because cities can do only what state legislatures expressly permit them to do (or what is "fairly implied" or "indispensable"), city charters often describe city powers in painstaking detail. For example, in the former city charter of Nashville, Tennessee, the replacement of regular members of the fire department above the rank of "pipeman" or "ladderman" (due to illness or disability) was spelled out so that there could be no mistake concerning the chain of command: the fire chief, subject to the mayor's approval, was to designate any regular member of the fire department from a lower rank to perform the duties of such member during his (or her) absence.

Even under home-rule charters (whereby cities can amend charters without going back to the legislature), cities are far from independent. They are still bound by the law of their state. And the state is omnipotent. In a 1923 case involving the city of Trenton and the state of New Jersey, the U.S. Supreme Court ruled that a state has the legal power to eliminate cities altogether, even against the will of the city's residents.

CHANGING RELATIONSHIPS

State Legislatures and City Interests

The posture of a state legislature is important to the cities of that state. Unfortunately for cities, historically, state legislatures generally adopted negative stances toward their cities—boxing them in with narrow grants of legal power and voting new power grudgingly.

City politicians have long felt victimized by their state legislatures. But the villains in the piece changed as the nation's population shifted from rural to urban to suburban locations. Specifically, before 1962, U.S. cities faced state legislatures dominated by rural, and usually antiurban, interests. By 1960, almost 70 percent of the U.S. population was urban, but about one-third of the states still had very large proportions of their population in rural areas. Further, before 1962 most state legislatures did not have the one person, one vote rule. Usually, state legislative districts were drawn so that rural voters could elect more than their proportional share of representatives. Before 1962, for example, only 11 percent of Californians (mainly from rural areas) could elect a majority of members of the California State Senate.

Beginning with a landmark Supreme Court case in 1962, *Baker v. Carr*, an ongoing process of reapportionment has been under way. This court decision required one person, one vote. It led to a redrawing of electoral district lines so that the population in all legislative districts is substantiality equal.

Since *Baker v. Carr* in 1962, rural domination of state legislatures has generally been reduced. But suburbs, not cities, have been the major benefactors. Demographics helps to explain why. By 1970, the U.S. population was roughly one-third urban, one-third suburban, and one-third rural or small town, with a slight suburban dominance. *(The share of the U.S. population living in suburbs doubled from 1900 to 1950. From 1950 to 2000, it doubled again. By 2000, the majority, 52 percent, of the U.S. population lived in suburbs.)*

The irony is this: State legislatures were reapportioned to ensure one person, one vote at the very time that population was shifting to the suburbs. Thus, reapportionment generally did not significantly benefit big cities. It did benefit suburbs and hurt rural areas.

In many states, a suburban–rural—antiurban coalition emerged in the 1970s, replacing the historic rural–antiurban coalition. This post-1970 antiurban coalition often voted (and continues to vote) against legislation designed to meet "big-city problems."

Antiurbanism escalated in the 1980s (and later, under a new name: "prosuburbanism"). By 1990, mounting budget deficits in state capitals forced many populous and suburban states, including California and Ohio, to make drastic cutbacks in welfare and education; these program cuts adversely affected more urbanities than suburbanites.

By the early 2000s, antiurbanism morphed into prosuburbanism. As discussed below, some members of the U.S. House of Representatives organized a "sub-urban agenda." Implicitly, this agenda pit the concerns of suburbanites against urbanites.

Suburbs Versus Cities

More than a generation ago, distinguished urban historian Richard C. Wade called suburbanization "the most important fact of American social and political life" since 1945 (1982:20). A number of analysts agree, noting a related fact: the emergence of two separate—and unequal—communities in the United States, suburbs and cities. (But, as we shall see, this clear separation has broken down in many U.S. metro areas, particularly when many inner suburbs suffer high poverty rates.)

Many suburbanites feel disconnected from (and fearful of) urban poverty, street crime, and other conditions facing their city neighbors—and more and more their *suburban* neighbors. Perhaps that is one reason more and more people are choosing gated communities, both in suburbs and in cities. (Suburban fear of urban poverty is rather ironic in the United States as, since 2005, the poverty rate in many close-in suburbs rivals or bests city rates.)

This emotional apartheid, based on suburban fear of city folk, can start very young. Student research teams in my classes at San Francisco State found, for instance, that children in suburban San Francisco held extremely negative views of the city. Although over 80 percent of the preteenage respondents had never visited San Francisco, they characterized the city as the home of crime, grime, and slime. The vast majority had nothing positive to say about San Francisco, the city voted—16 years in a row—by readers of a U.S. travel magazine as their top destination (Thousman, 2008).

Perhaps it is no accident, then, that Orlando, Florida, home of Disney World's Magic Kingdom (claiming 15.4 million visitors in 2000)—not San Francisco, "everyone's favorite city," or any national park or New York City or Los Angeles—is the most popular vacation destination in the United States. It is also noteworthy that the top destination in the United States by motorcoach in one post-millennium year, 2001, was Branson, Missouri. As a *New York Times* reporter put it years earlier when Branson started its rise, "the astounding growth of this squeaky-clean, virtually all-white, middle-of-nowhere Mecca is a revealing slice of America." One tourist at Branson's Elvis-A-Rama and glitzy country music theaters revealed why he vacationed there rather than in Los Angeles: "There's no smog blowing down from the hillsides. There's no graffiti. There are no gangs. I'm not prejudiced, but it's nice to be someplace where everyone speaks English" (in Applebome, 1993:B1).

Recent Suburban Antiurbanism in the United States

Suburban-city antipathy remains, despite the suburbanization of poverty and other so-called urban problems that now are part of suburban life. Indeed, months before they lost control of the U.S. House of Representatives in 2006, Republicans organized a "suburban agenda." Fifty members of the House of Representatives, all representing suburbs and all Republican, joined the Suburban Agenda Caucus. Here is what one Caucus member, Congressperson Mike Castle (R-Del.), wrote on his blog in May 2006:

DELAWARE COMMUNITIES ARE OFTEN CONSIDERED SUBURBS OF THE MAJOR CITIES THAT SURROUND US—SUCH AS WILMINGTON, BALTIMORE AND PHILADELPHIA. IT IS WHERE MANY FAMILIES RESIDE AND WHERE CONCERNS ABOUT OPEN SPACE, EDUCATION AND HEALTH CARE ARE TOP ON RESIDENTS' MINDS. BECAUSE OF THIS, I JOINED THE SUBURBAN AGENDA CAUCUS IN THE HOUSE OF REPRESENTATIVES, COMPRISED OF 50 MEMBERS REPRESENTING SUBURBAN AREAS, FROM WASHINGTON STATE TO FLORIDA. WE RECENTLY UNVEILED A NEW FAMILY AGENDA FOR CONGRESS THAT WILL FOCUS ON ADDRESSING THE NEEDS AND PRIORITIES OF SUBURBAN COMMUNITIES THROUGHOUT THE UNITED STATES. THE CAUCUS IS PUSHING INDIVIDUAL BILLS BACKED BY VOTERS IN SUBURBAN AREAS INCLUDING 401 KIDS SAVINGS ACCOUNTS, HEALTH INFORMATION TECHNOLOGY, OPEN SPACE CONSERVATION AND INTERNET PROTECTION FOR KIDS.

(CASTLE, 2006)

Was Congressperson Castle asserting that city folk are *not* concerned with such "family agenda" issues as open space, education, and health care? Or was this suburban agenda, poll-tested in 22 suburban counties, more about winning elections in mainly formerly Republican districts on the edge of big cities?

The head of the Suburban Caucus, a Republican from Chicago's northern suburbs, argued that the suburban agenda was neither Democratic nor Republican: "It comes out of suburban thinking" (in James, 2006). Some close observers disagreed. Two *Chicago Tribune* reporters called the suburban agenda an election ploy by Republicans to appeal to suburban voters, many of whom were Democratic voters who had left cities for inner suburbs (Zeleny and Kuzcka in James, 2006). If so, the ploy didn't work very well: Republicans lost control of the House, and the losses included six caucus members. (The losses had less to do with the suburban agenda than with other issues, including the Iraq War, inappropriate sexual behavior with under age boys [Mark Foley, R-Fla.], and an FBI investigation [Curt Weld, R-Pa.].)

In the past generation, so many urbanites moved to the suburbs that, by 2000, the *majority* of people in the United States lived around central cities, not in them. Movers' reasons varied widely. One key reason concerned a desire to flee—from city people, from city "problems," and/or from paying for public programs to address those problems. Radical observer Mike Davis (1993) calls this attitude "the War against the Cities." I call it the "moating and gating of suburban America" or the "Yes, you *can* run and hide" syndrome. Whatever it's called, it describes suburban antiurbanism.

What lies behind this suburban antiurbanism? Analysts disagree. *Chicago Tribune* Washington bureau chief Frank James (2006) implies that race—whites vs. people of color—is all-important. James points to the thinly veiled "us" vs. "them" comments by a member of the Republican Suburban Caucus:

YOU KNOW, THE FEDERAL GOVERNMENT HAS ALL KINDS OF PROGRAMS FOR OUR CITIES....WE DEVOTE TONS OF RESOURCES TO OUR CITIES AS WELL WE SHOULD....BUT OFTENTIMES IT SEEMS TO THE PEOPLE WHO LIVE IN THE SUBURBS THAT IT IS DONE AT THEIR EXPENSE.

(JAMES, 2006)

Reporter James comments that this congressperson's words could easily be seen as an appeal to white voters: "Since cities tend to have higher percentages of African Americans and other minorities than many suburbs, [the Caucus Congressperson's] comments could certainly be interpreted as an attempt to capitalize on white voters' flawed perceptions that blacks and other minorities receive most federal funding."

Radical iconoclast Mike Davis (1993) sees race and conservative politics as the keys to suburban antiurbanism. According to Davis, a conservative coalition in Congress united suburban and rural representatives in both major political parties against any federal reinvestment in big cities dominated by minorities. Indeed, he charges that all major candidates for president in 1992 may have acted "in cynical concert to exclude a subject [from their debates] that had become mutually embarrassing—cities": "The word 'city' now color-coded and worrisome to the candidates' common suburban heartland—was expunged from the exchanges. Thus the elephant of the urban crisis was simply. . .conjured out of sight" (3). Davis concludes that the 1992 presidential election showed that "the big cities, once the very fulcrum of the political universe during Franklin Roosevelt's presidency, have been demoted to the status of a scorned and impotent electoral periphery" (3).

(Bringing Davis's argument forward, cities have remained a non-issue in all U.S. presidential elections since. However, some think—or hope—that postelection "realities" of President Obama's United States, such as the desire to decrease unemployment in part by fixing infrastructure, may change that.)

Public-opinion analyst William Schneider also attributes suburban antiurbanism to conservative ideology. Schneider claims that "a major reason people move out to the suburbs is simply to be able to buy their own government. These people resent it when politicians take their money and use it to solve other people's problems, especially when they don't believe that government can actually solve those problems" (1992:38).

"Urbanization of the Suburbs"

Yet, ironies abound. First, some U.S. suburbs *look* more like inner cities than stereotypical, upper middle- and upper-class, pale-faced suburbs, such as the one depicted in the film *American Beauty* (1999). Second, suburban poverty is not an oxymoron. Indeed, in 2005, for the first time in U.S. history, poor suburbanites outnumbered poor urbanites in the nation's 100 biggest metro areas. According to Brookings Institution analysts Berube and Kneebone (2006), *over 12 million people in U.S. suburbs of the 100 most populated metropolitan areas were defined as poor while fewer—11 million—urbanites in those same metro areas were defined as poor.*

This new reality of more suburban than urban poor in the largest U.S. metro areas could/should change stereotypes: Big cities are usually seen as home to the nation's poor, surrounded by suburbs populated by middle- and upper-income residents. Yet, U.S. suburbs are more diverse in terms of race and class than ever before. One reason: Increasing numbers of recent immigrants (whose incomes tend to be lower than native-born U.S. residents) are settling in suburbs, not cities—particularly in the South and the West.

In addition, many suburbs now face so-called big-city problems, such as rising crime, low-paying jobs, and low-performing schools. In 2006, the president of the National Urban League (Morial in Associated Press, 2006) called it "the urbanization of the suburbs." (Surely, he was referring to this sense of the word "urbanization," as the process of becoming urban in terms of social, technological, political, and spatial organization.)

I think there is another important factor behind antiurbanism: widespread pessimism about the future. Citizens seem resigned to diminishing expectations and urban (and suburban) decline. This feeling is rooted in global shifts that affect people in suburbs, cities, and rural areas, albeit differently.

Historically, and for good reason, people in the United States were optimistic after World War II: They had rising expectations for the national economy and their own fortunes. Especially if they were white, they expected that their children would live with more, not less, than they had. Even without having heard of Burgess's hypothesis, they understood that moving *out* to the suburbs meant moving *up*. Literally millions of white middle-class and working-class people in the United States left town in the 1950s and beyond.

But by the 1970s and early 1980s, global economic restructuring hit home. Once secure and relatively high-paid jobs in manufacturing moved to cheaper labor areas. Few high-paid jobs replaced them. White-collar and no-collar (digirati) workers, including top managers, also felt insecure as companies merged or went "offshore," and they found themselves unemployed or "rightsized" out of work. Consequently, for ever-increasing numbers, future prosperity seemed dreamlike.

By the early 1990s, people in the United States were wondering what had gone wrong. Increasingly, many were satisfied if they could keep their income and living standards from declining.

In sum, downward mobility was knocking at the door. What does this have to do with suburban antiurbanism? Probably a great deal. During boom times, it is easier to have compassion for—or at least neutrality toward—strangers and people unlike oneself (or assumed to be different). During gloomy economic times, the politics of resentment can grip the heart and purse, widening the gulf between "us" and "them." The newly-insecure

TABLE 4.3A, B | *The World's Largest Incorporated Suburbs, Two Views*

TABLE 4.3A.*

Rank	City	Population	Metropolitan Area	Nation	Source
1	Giza	2,221,868	Greater Cairo	Egypt	Egypt Census, 1996
2	Quezon City	2,173,831	Metro Manila	Philippines	Philippines Census 2002
3	Bekasi	1,931,976	Greater Jakarta	Indonesia	Indonesia Census 2000
4	Ecatepec de Morelos	1,688,258	Greater Mexico City	Mexico	Mexico Census 2005 CONAPO
5	Kobe	1,528,940	Greater Osaka	Japan	Japan Oct. 2006
6	Tangerang	1,488,666	Greater Jakarta	Indonesia	Indonesia Census 2000
7	Depok	1,353,249	Greater Jakarta	Indonesia	Indonesia Census 2000
8	Kawasaki	1,342,232	Greater Tokyo	Japan	Japan Oct. 2006
9	Guarulhos	1,283,253	Greater São Paulo	Brazil	Brazil IBGE Estimate 2006
10	Thana	1,261,517	Greater Mumbai	India	India Census 2001

*Does not include cities that require exact records of birth, death, and moving, such as in Japan and Brazil, which estimate city populations annually.

TABLE 4.3B

Rank	City	Population	Metropolitan Area	Nation	Source
1	Bekasi	1,931,976	Greater Jakarta, Jabotabek	Indonesia	Indonesia Census 2000
2	Ecatepec de Morelos	1,688,258	Greater Mexico City	Mexico	Mexico Census 2005 CONAPO
3	Tangerang	1,488,666	Greater Jakarta, Jabotabek	Indonesia	Indonesia Census 2000
4	Depok	1,353,249	Greater Jakarta, Jabotabek	Indonesia	Indonesia Census 2000
5	Kawasaki	1,342,232	Greater Tokyo Area	Japan	Japan Oct. 2006
6	Guarulhos	1,283,253	Greater São Paulo	Brazil	Brazil IBGE Estimate 2006
7	Thana	1,261,517	Greater Mumbai	India	India Census 2001
8	Kalyan	1,193,266	Greater Mumbai	India	India Census 2001
9	Saitama	1,182,000	Greater Tokyo	Japan	Japan Census 2005
10	Caloocan	1,177,604	Metro Manila	Philippines	Philippines Census 2002

Source of Indonesian and Indian population data is citypopulation.de.

often assign blame to someone or something for their falling fortunes, not to global processes beyond their control. In this milieu, many fled to gated communities or "safer" suburbs rather than fight what they saw as irreversible urban decline, especially dangerous streets.

Liberals would say that the well-off blame the victims. Conservatives would say that the well-off rightly blame those who have not helped themselves but prefer to live off government giveaways. Marxist radicals would say that it is ironic. A group of better-off people blame those at the bottom of the social ladder instead of the structures of capitalism that tend to impoverish them both.

Meantime, we should remember that the term "suburb" covers many types of communities. In Europe, many inner suburbs are populated by lower-income immigrants, including large percentages of underemployed or unemployed who live in high-rise tenements. And, as Table 4.3a and b show, many global "suburbs" have more residents than cities considered large in the United States (even if scholars disagree on exactly which suburbs are the largest in the world).

In the United States, the *stereotypical* suburb is a bedroom community of upper-income, mainly or all-white areas beyond the city limits. It features well-manicured lawns and single-family homes, such as those on Wisteria Lane, the home of TV's *Desperate Housewives*.

Yet, U.S. suburbs are much more diverse racially, socially, and economically. The range of suburbs in the United States is considerable: from poor white suburbs; predominantly middle-class African American suburbs; older, shabby industrial suburbs; mixed-use suburbs; rich residential suburbs, and lower-income Latino suburbs (e.g., Huntington Park outside Los Angeles, Berwyn and Stone Park in suburban Chicago) to Asian-dominant suburbs such as Los Angeles's Monterey Park, whose 2000 population was more than 40 percent Chinese American and over 60 percent Asian and Asian American, including Vietnamese and Korean, with a substantial number living in poverty.

In the past two decades or so, particularly in larger metro areas, there has been an upsurge of new ethnic, suburban residents. Activities to serve them often follow but not at the expense of non-ethnicity-based activities. For example, in one upscale Boston suburb with increased numbers of Chinese Americans, in recent years it has not been unusual to come upon a scene like this: "Between reciting Chinese poetry and performing traditional dance routines, [Chinese American] kids munched on McDonald's fries and hunched over Game Boy consoles" (Noonan, 2007).

In the past two decades or so, there have been other momentous city-suburban changes. Importantly, poverty has moved into the suburbs in a big way. In the 100 biggest U.S. metro areas, suburban poverty now outranks urban poverty in terms of numbers of people affected. (Note, however, that the poverty *rate* in U.S. big cities [18.4 percent] remains higher than in their close-in suburbs [9.4 percent].)

Given that many feel that the future portends fewer, not more, property owners, U.S. suburbanites seek to hold the line economically. This condition makes them very tax-sensitive. The upshot is often suburban hostility, particularly in suburbs farther from the urban core, to both government and cities. This hostility coincides with two recent sociospatial developments that have important political consequences:

1. Since 1990, suburban residents are a majority in many states, including the nation's largest, California.

2. Many suburbanites live in edge cities or post-suburbia, settlements that are no longer dependent economically and socially on the urban core.

In brief, scarcity—not familiarity—can breed contempt. Fear can also breed secession from the union—not of South or Sunbelt from North and Rustbelt but of outer suburbs from the urban core. With little hope for a more prosperous future and no sense of community with their urban neighbors, suburbanites are not anxious to share their tax dollars with urban strangers.

Yet, ironically, many suburbs share city-type problems, including poverty, as already noted. As many Big City mayors have long held, a city's problems cannot be walled in. For example, affluent suburban counties around New York City face congestion, drugs, crime, expensive housing, garbage mounds, air pollution, and other so-called urban problems. Further, according to the U.S. Bureau of Justice Statistics, in 2005, urbanites did have the highest violent victimization rates, but suburbanites were far from crime-free. For example, six urbanites, four suburbanites, and four rural residents per 1,000 were victims of aggravated assault (Bureau of Justice Statistics, 2009).

Nonetheless, few suburbanites apparently see a common future with their urban neighbors. Not do those seeking high political office. For more than a quarter-century, perhaps reflecting the demographic shift to the suburbs, no U.S. presidential candidate has addressed specifically urban issues.

So, if you mix economic insecurity, fear for personal safety on city streets, and tense race relations with long-standing cynicism about government, what have you got? A recipe for a volatile brew. Depending on your ideology and optimism-pessimism quotient, you see either (1) the new survival of the fittest, (2) creative challenges, or (3) the war of all against all.

It is noteworthy that when issues are not framed as urban-suburban, U.S. suburbanites seem to follow the Golden Rule. Take health care, for example. One national random sample poll in 2007 (Roberts, 2007) revealed that a vast majority of respondents favored coverage for everyone, presumably urbanites as well as suburbanites and rural dwellers. Similarly, a 2008 poll (*Rasmussen Reports*, 2008) found that 67 percent of respondents thought that the same level of insurance coverage available to members of Congress should be available to everyone. (Note that neither poll asked respondents if they were willing to pay more money to cover insurance for everyone. A poll years earlier did find that suburbanites said they would pay for urban dwellers to be insured.)

To summarize: U.S. cities are creatures of state law. States can grant or take away powers from cities at will. State legislatures spell out city powers in general laws or charters. In some states, cities are granted considerable discretion to determine their own structures and powers under home-rule charters, but even home-rule cities are far from independent. Furthermore, cities have been under the domination of state legislatures, historically controlled by rural interests and antiurban attitudes.

Demographic shifts and reapportionment reduced rural domination. But ironically, suburbs—not cities—gained the most influence and power from these changes. Unhappily for cities, suburban dominance, combined with economic hard times and fiscal austerity, led to a new and grimmer round of antiurbanism.

Local Governments in a Global Society

"TAKING RESPONSIBILITY FOR THE SKY"

"All politics is local." This maxim, often attributed to the late speaker of the U.S. House of Representatives Tip O'Neill, means that local interests mold national political issues. Closing a naval base, for example, may be influenced by the local unemployment rate and the clout of the district's congressperson.

But there is another sort of local politics, and it works in reverse: It starts locally and spreads. For instance, the city council of Irvine, a city in postsuburban Orange County, California, passed legislation restricting chlorofluorocarbons (CFCs) in the city. The anti-CFC ordinance raised the cost of some goods for local residents and caused hardships for some businesses. Indeed, it seemed idealistic, even quixotic, for one city council to try to solve the ozone depletion situation and to take responsibility for the sky. So why did they do it? Perhaps the idea of locality takes on renewed importance as global problems feel over-whelming, and political awareness can lead to a feeling of helplessness if some action isn't taken. Perhaps they asked themselves, "If not us, who?" and refused to accept the answer of "Nobody."

Not a prairie fire but at least a flashlight, the action of one city, Irvine, illuminated the actions of other localities. Indeed, many other places, from California and New York to Japan's Shiga Prefecture, have taken responsibility for the sky. . .and the earth. . .and the water. . .and their fellow beings. In Detroit, 125 teenagers and young adults worked with local residents to rehabilitate houses and march against crack houses as part of a Green Cities project. Two communities, one in Japan and the other in Siberia, have a "sister lake" relationship; they jointly study the flight of birds that migrate to and from their areas. And so on.

To conclude: Local actions—from passing anti-pollution and gun-control ordinances to conducting municipal foreign policy—have wider political significance. Such local deeds not only encourage collective action but also signal local resistance to the power of the nation-state.

FORMS OF CITY GOVERNMENT

Globally, forms and functions of municipal government differ widely—from Bolivia's elected mayors and councils and Bangladesh's (proposed) four-tier system to the (mega)city-state of Singapore, with its three tiered local system. Since 1990, many sub-national governments have undergone fundamental transformation. For example, before 1990, most countries in East Asia were highly centralized, but now local or regional governments from China to Thailand are responsible for delivering some critical services and economic development.

Some comments and concepts we will discuss (e.g., know-who) may or may not apply to local governments globally. Given space constraints, here we will discuss only forms of city government in the United States.

As suggested, the first step in understanding how U.S. cities (including suburban cities) work is to clarify the city-state relationship. The second step entails understanding how a city's internal government is structured.

Getting something done in a city takes know-how and *know-who*. Who has the authority to condemn an unsafe building? What bureaucrat can grant a permit to hold a rally in the park? Can the mayor fire the school superintendent who has ordered the closing of the high school for his own birthday? Knowing whom to go to and how to get something done begins with an understanding of a city's governmental form.

Most U.S. city governments fall into one of three categories: the mayor-council form, the council-manager form, and the commission form. (In New England, town meetings also exist; they are used mainly by cities with less than 10,000 population and exclusively by cities with fewer than 100,000 inhabitants.) Large U.S. cities generally have a mayor-council form. Some smaller cities also follow this model.

However, many smaller and medium-sized communities, particularly metropolitan suburbs that grew up in the last century, have a city council-manager form. Here, a city manager, appointed by the city council and accountable to that legislative body, plays a key leadership role, and the elected mayor is less important.

Finally, some cities have a commission form of government. Here, elected commissioners act collectively as the city council and individually as heads of city departments.

Mayor-Council Form

The **mayor-council form** is the most common form of city government in the United States. It is also the predominant form in large cities. The organization chart in Figure 4.1 shows that under this form of government mayors typically have appointment power—that is, they can appoint department heads. They do not have this power in council-manager cities.

The organization chart also shows that the mayor and city council are elected independently. The mayor's independent elected status and significant appointment power indicate that under the mayor-council form mayors have important executive powers. Other factors, not revealed on the organization chart, contribute to the mayor's role as executive leader. These may include the ability to intervene directly in the conduct of city government operations, to veto the city's budget, and to initiate legislation.

Council–Manager Form

Consider Figure 4.2. The fact that the mayor is in a box, somewhere off in left field, is a significant feature of the **council–manager form of government**. Under this form, which is common in many medium-sized U.S. communities, the mayor has much less power and authority than in a mayor–council government. The

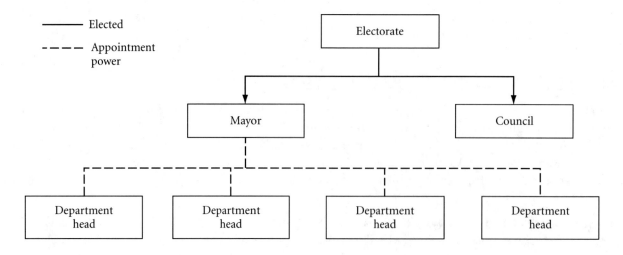

FIG. 4.1 | *The Mayor-Council Form of Local Government in the United States.*

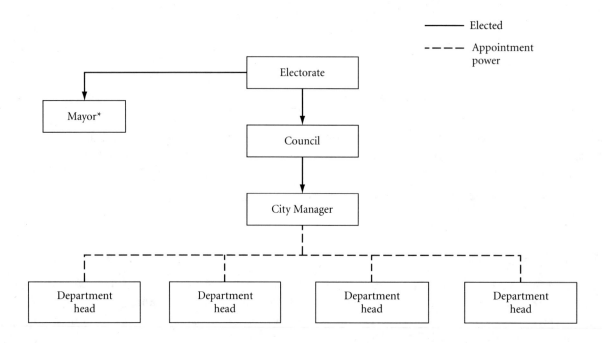

FIG. 4.2 | *The Council–Manager Form of Local Government in the United States.*
Independently elected or appointed from among the council members.

important actor in this fairly recent form of government is the **city manager**, appointed by the city council, as Figure 4.2 indicates. Usually, the manager serves at the pleasure of the elected city council and can be removed at any time if a majority of councillors so decide. The city manager, in turn, typically has the power to hire and fire heads of city departments. He or she is also responsible for preparing the city budget, developing policy recommendations for the council's action, and overseeing city government.

In many cities, the city manager draws a bigger salary than the mayor or council members (who may be part-time or amateur administrators). Further, the city manager has a larger personal staff and more control over the

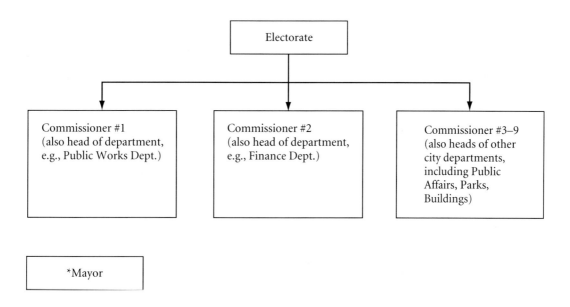

FIG. 4.3 | *The Commission Form of Local Government in the United States.*

Usually appointed from among commissioners.

flow of information than the mayor or councillors. This combination of professional expertise and access to and control over information gives city managers informal power beyond what is revealed in organization charts.

Commission Form

Under the **commission form of government**, voters elect a relatively small number of commissioners, who play a dual role as legislators and executives. Commissioners approve legislation and also head the city's departments.

The commission form was introduced in Galveston, Texas, following a flood in 1900 that left the city and its finances under water. Today, no U.S. city with a population over 500,000 operates under this form—for good reasons. As Figure 4.3 shows, there is no strong executive leader. Power is exercised collectively by the city commissioners—the parks commissioner, police commissioner, and so on. Historically, this ideal of collective leadership has resulted in lack of coordination and government by amateurs.

To conclude: Few cities today use the commission form, the mayor–council structure predominates in larger cities, and council–manager governments are most commonly found in medium-sized cities and suburbs. Why is the council–manager form so attractive to medium-sized communities and so unattractive to large cities? To understand this, some background is necessary.

The city manager plan was initiated in Staunton, Virginia, in 1908. It spread slowly throughout the nation up to the 1940s. After World War II, the council–manager form became widespread in medium-sized communities, especially upper-income, white suburbs. Generally speaking, these suburbanites thought that the council-manager form would ensure professional, businesslike government and guard against something defined as inefficient, unprofessional, and corrupt: big-city politics. Many observers think that council–manager governments are best suited to relatively homogeneous white-collar communities. Why? Because there the political representation of diverse interests is not important. Thus, ordinarily we shouldn't expect to find a city manager running a city composed of various ethnic groups and a significant blue-collar population. Typically, mayors operate in cities that mediate among diverse interests, not cities that seek primarily to create pleasant living conditions.

ORGANIZATION OF CITY GOVERNMENTS

Mayors, Strong or Weak

In U.S. cities with mayor–council governments, the **mayor** is popularly considered to be the head of city government, the responsible official with whom the local buck stops. But as the song says, "It ain't necessarily so." Often, a mayor is powerless to improve bus service, create jobs for the unemployed, or reorganize the delivery of city services. Although decades old, the following exchange before a congressional committee between then U.S. Senator Abraham Ribicoff (D.-Conn.) and then mayor of Los Angeles, Sam Yorty, is instructive:

Senator Ribicoff: As I listened to your testimony, Mayor Yorty, I made some notes. This morning you have really waived authority and responsibility in the following areas: schools, welfare, transportation, employment, health, and housing, which leaves you as head of a city with a ceremonial function, police, and recreation.

Mayor Yorty: That is right, and fire.

Senator Ribicoff: And fire.

Mayor Yorty: Yes.

Senator Ribicoff: Collecting sewage?

Mayor Yorty: Sanitation; that is right.

Senator Ribicoff: In other words, basically you lack jurisdiction, authority, responsibility for what makes a city move?

Mayor Yorty: That is exactly it. (U.S. Senate, 1966–1967:774)

In this exchange, Senator Ribicoff seems to blame Mayor Yorty for "waiving" responsibility. But in fact, Yorty never had the responsibility. Then, as now, in Los Angeles (and many other cities), mayors have limited powers, making them weak chief executives. Nonetheless, as outgoing San Francisco Mayor Dianne Feinstein (and later U.S. senator) warned her successor, "Anytime there's trouble, whether [the] Muni[cipal railway] breaks down or someone is cited for double parking, they all come to you. There is no Teflon with this job" (1988:5).

Under the weak mayor–council arrangement, the city council or independent administrative boards dominate city decision making. Further, mayors (either strong or weak) have no authority to control many independent units of government within their political boundaries (e.g., school districts), as we shall soon see.

In weak-mayor governments, administrative boards or commissions exercise power independently of the mayor (who typically appoints members and can remove them). This arrangement serves to broaden the base of political participation. Indeed, city boards are often appointed with a keen eye on local power blocs. In San Francisco, for example, members of appointed boards reflect the city's ethnic and cultural pluralism. They are composed of a mix of African Americans, whites, Latinos, Asian Americans, single parents, labor unionists, real estate brokers, gays and lesbians, environmentalists, and so forth.

Weak or strong, mayors often have little discretion over city money. In San Francisco, for example, the mayor controls only about 30 cents out of every budget dollar. The rest has to be spent on programs mandated by federal and state government, such as health care and jails.

Hyperpluralism and Government by Bureaucrats

A weak-mayor form of government is attractive to many citizens because it can lead to a government that is responsive to diverse interest groups. But does it lead to responsible government? No, say many political scientists. Years ago, Frederick Wirt made a strong case for the idea that the costs of the weak-mayor form outweigh its benefits.

Political scientist Wirt (1971:114) argued that the price paid for decentralized, fractionated power in a pluralistic city is an inability to formulate and implement long-range public policy. Wirt argued that if successful policy outcomes rest on the agreement of many disparate private groups and public authorities, the power of one component to block any action is magnified. The result, he said, is that over time only minor policy adjustments are possible.

According to Wirt, the result of so many disparate actors playing the political game is **hyperpluralism**. Having too many (*hyper*) different decision points and too many groups with veto power (*pluralism*) paralyzes public policymaking. The result, Wirt said, is non-decision making.

In the absence of strong executive leadership and the presence of disparate competing factions, who runs a heterogeneous U.S. city? According to Wirt, the bureaucrats take over. He claimed that the result is a "government by clerks": long-staying, professional civil servants who were never elected and thus can't be recalled. They may be regulated by professional norms of service and efficiency, but they're not accountable to the citizenry. (*Note*: Unlike Wirt, some think that a "government by clerks"—composed of a competent and loyal bureaucracy—is not such a bad option.)

The growing strength of municipal unions further erodes city executives' power and authority. Max Weber predicted what some call the *bureaucratic phenomenon*—the rise and expansion of rational but fearsome bureaucratic administration and politics.

Decades ago, many studies of big-city politics found decision making there to be hopelessly fractionated (e.g., Sayre and Kaufman, 1960). Today, some wonder if cities are ungovernable; they ask whether or not there are any solutions to unresponsive bureaucracies, proliferating and competing interest groups, weak control over public employees, and dwindling fiscal resources. But others argue that bureaucracies can become responsive, and communities can be empowered if only the entrepreneurial spirit is introduced. And still others have a different slant altogether. They claim that it doesn't matter if bureaucrats or bosses run the town; neither is accountable to the citizens, and neither has the interests of most citizens in mind. Among other things, what is needed, they say, is more citizen participation and grassroots organizing.

To conclude: The formal structure of government limits leadership. Weak mayors have a hard time providing executive leadership and gathering resources to meet urban needs. Even strong mayors, who have more authority to meet some urban needs, can't control many key policy areas that have an impact on the quality of life in their cities. Nonetheless, mayors—weak or strong—bear the brunt of public dismay when trouble occurs.

Given their limited legal power, weak mayors must use informal powers to push through their programs. These include the power to persuade, the support of public opinion, and, in some cases, the influence that comes from controlling a well-oiled political machine. (Box 4.1 outlines some factors that make a mayor weak or strong.)

THE CONTEXT OF LOCAL GOVERNMENT

I have hinted at one reason that U.S. mayors are unable to govern effectively: They can't control other units of government. Both strong and weak mayors operate in the context of a fragmented metropolis and a global economy.

Fragmentation of the Metropolis

To paraphrase Abraham Lincoln (who once commented that "God must love the common man, he made so many of them" (see Cyber National International, 1997–2003), we could say that God must have loved cities too because She or He made so many of them. Over the decades this has remained the case. Indeed, there are more, not fewer, units of most local government in the United States now than 20 or 30 years ago. (The big exception is school districts, greatly consolidated since the 1950s.) By July 30, 2002, there were 87,849 units of

Legal Structure

Strong	Weak

Strong

1. Mayor–council plan, which grants the mayor the following powers in the city charter:
   a. A 4-year term of office with possible reelection for many terms
   b. Power to appoint and remove city commissioners and/or department heads at will
   c. Power over the city budget (e.g., the right to submit an executive budget or have veto power over items in the budget)

Weak

1. Council–manager or commission form of government with only a ceremonial role for the mayor

2. Mayor–council plan, in which the city charter limits the mayor's power in the following ways:
   a. A short term of office (e.g., 2 years)
   b. Commissioners and department heads not subject to the mayor's authority (e.g., commissioners appointed by the city council, agency heads protected by civil service)
   c. Little or no authority over budget matters

Local Government Context

Strong

1. State constitution and/or general laws and/or city charter provisions do not significantly limit city authority

2. City performs many important local government functions

Weak

1. State constitution and/or general law and/or city charter provisions limit city authority significantly

2. Other layers of government (county, special districts, etc.)

Personal Power and Influence

Strong

1. An effective political organization (e.g., a well-oiled political machine)

2. Strong support from powerful local interests, such as the financial/business community or labor

Weak

1. A weak or substantially nonexistent political organization

2. Lack of support from powerful local interests

local government. Of these, 38,971 were general-purpose local governments—3,034 county governments and 35,937 subcounty governments, including 19,431 municipal governments. The rest, over 50 percent of the total, were "special-purpose" local governments, including 13,522 school districts (a significant drop from 67,355 in 1952) and 35,356 special districts (see Table 4.4).

To further complicate matters, local government is organized in a crazy quilt pattern of separate and often overlapping types. To unravel the intricacies of this crazy quilt, some basic vocabulary is necessary. **Municipality** is the U.S. Census Bureau's term for general-purpose units of local government. Cities are general-purpose governments; that is, they undertake a variety of functions and provide a range of services. Hence, by definition, *cities are municipalities. Towns, townships, and boroughs are also municipalities.* Other units of local government—separate from municipalities—include school districts, other special districts, and counties. *Fragmentation, proliferation,* and *Balkanization* are terms often used to refer to this pattern of local government.

TABLE 4.4 | *Special Districts, by Function, 2002*

Function	Number
Total	35,356
Total single-function districts	32,157
Natural resources	7,026
Fire protection	5,743
Water supply	3,423
Housing and community development	3,413
Sewerage	2,020
Cemeteries	1,670
Libraries	1,582
Parks and recreation	1,314
Highways	767
Health	743
Hospitals	735
Education	530
Airports	512
Utilities other than water supply	485
Other	2,194
Multiple-function districts	3,199

Source: Adapted from Table D. p. 7, U.S. Census Bureau, July 2002 (http://ftp2.census.gov/govs/cog/2002COGprelim_report.pdf).

This is the way the crazy quilt of local government is patterned within a Metropolitan Statistical Area (MSA): Cities and other municipalities lie within the boundaries of a county. Within city boundaries (and often extending beyond them) are school districts and various other special districts that are independent of the city. Each unit of government—county, city, special district, school district—is a separate legal entity. This is important for analyzing how local government operates.

Special Districts

Special districts are the most widespread type of local government in the United States, and their number keeps growing. As of 2002, there were 35,356 special-district governments; in 1942, there were only 8,299.

One of three types of "special-purpose governments" (the others are corporations and authorities) in the United States, they are set up to serve either a single purpose (e.g., sewage treatment, housing–community development, hospital services, or fire protection) or several purposes, such as sewage and water provision.

Directors of special districts are not accountable to city or county government officials because special districts are totally separate legal entities. Their boundaries do not necessarily conform to those of any other local government unit. Often, they overlap the boundaries of the city and each other.

The existence of independent, overlapping special districts can create problems for the coordination of public services. In one unincorporated area of Portland, Oregon, for example, 11 separate special districts provide various services to area residents. No boundaries of these 11 special districts are contiguous. Some residents live within the borders of one district but just outside the borders of another. Further, each of the 11 districts has its own governing body, which is totally separate from all other local government units. Uncoordinated services can result if sewer district supervisors use plan A for digging ditches while water district supervisors use plan B for supplying water.

Many states have attempted to limit the proliferation of special districts and to consolidate existing ones. These efforts have met with only limited success.

Why are special districts so popular? The main reason is that special districts are separate from other local governments and, thus, not subject to their debt limits. Special districts can issue bonds or borrow money after other local governments have reached the legal limits of their borrowing authority. For example, residents who want more sewers in a city that has already reached its debt limt might form an independent sewer district. The new special district could sell bonds to finance the sewer construction, unrestricted by the city debt limit. Also, districts can be drawn around a functional area, regardless of local government boundaries A mosquito-abatement district may cover the swampy part of three cities.

Counties (Including Urban Counties)

Historically, the **county** has proved to be very stable unit of government; its boundaries have generally remained unchanged for decades. For this reason, the county is used by the U.S. Census Bureau as the basic unit of the MSA.

In rural areas where there are no incorporated cities, county government acts as the general-purpose local government; typically, it regulates land use, licenses businesses, and provides police and fire protection. In urban areas, cities usually take over the basic general-purpose local government functions for their residents. In urban areas, counties serve as the general-purpose local government only for the unincorporated territory that lies within them. Counties also may provide some services to the residents of cities within their boundaries. For example, frequently the county operates libraries within both cities and unincorporated areas.

In recent times, a new spatial–demographic entity has emerged: the **urban county**. This term is used in various ways. It may refer to (1) a county that has assumed comprehensive authority over governmental functions, as in the case of Miami-Dade County, Florida; (2) any county with a large, dense population, giving it the characteristics of a city; or (3) a county that meets specified population size and legal power requirements to be eligible for certain federal funds.

Urban counties will probably become increasingly important. Recognizing this, some states have passed legislation that treats urban counties essentially as cities.

The State's Role in Urban Affairs

Apart from their formal legal power, states exert power and authority over cities in many ways. For example, state programs operate within a city's boundaries, and cities may have little or no influence on these programs. Highway construction is illustrative. A state-funded highway can dramatically affect local land use, industrial location, and housing. Yet those cities through which it passes have no voice in determining its route.

The level of state involvement with urban issues varies widely. After the War on Poverty and other Great Society programs of the 1960s, U.S. statehouses were often bypassed by federal grants directly to city halls or neighborhood groups, thus decreasing state clout over their cities. However, some states have taken an active role, creating institutions to deal with their cities.

To summarize: City governments are only one of several units of local government in the United States. Counties, school districts, and other special districts also exist, often performing city-like functions. In MSAs, there is a crazy quilt of fragmented and overlapping municipalities, counties, school districts, and other special districts. Some states also play a significant role in local affairs.

Areawide Planning Efforts

In theory, the variety and vast array of decentralized local governments ensure citizens a democratic voice in matters that directly affect their lives. In practice, however, things are quite different.

For one thing, voters have little or no control over the most widespread of all local governments: the special district. Critics charge that supervisors of special districts often put special interests, particularly private business, or technical concerns above the public interest. Influential labor negotiator Theodore W. Kheel, for one argued that the Port Authority of New York and New Jersey (a multistate special district which owned the World Trade Center) is dominated by the interests of its corporate bondholders. In effect, Kheel said, the Port Authority serves the rich and is indifferent to the needs of people in the New York City area (Kheel, [1969] 1971:443–449).

For another thing, many local issues, particularly land-use and economic growth policies, have area-wide effects. If city A permits a large chemical factory to locate there, nearby cities can be affected (by pollution, new transport patterns, etc.). But the affected cities have no say in the matter. Thus, the crazy-quilt pattern of fragmented local government appears to give metropolitan residents the worst of both worlds: little democratic control and lack of coordinated policies.

Pushed largely by federal government requirements or incentives, most MSAs have established some kind of metropolitanwide planning organization. These organizations, called either a **council of governments (COG)** or an **areawide planning organization**, are strictly voluntary and advisory. Local governments are not legally required to follow their recommendations. Consequently, COGs operate on good will. And sometimes good will runs smack into a fiscal crunch or serious political disagreement. The case of a large COG, the Association of Bay Area Governments (ABAG), is instructive. ABAG is the land-use planning agency for the nine-county San Francisco Bay Area, and by some accounts, it is a powerful lobbying group. Besides conducting research and advising on water quality and other matters, ABAG sets mandates for low-income housing.

Do COGs represent the wave of the future for interlocal cooperation and areawide coordination? Not likely. To date, most have been little more than intergovernmental talk shows: Views are expressed, but nothing much happens—unless the going gets rough. Then, cities and other local governments walk out. (Example: Years ago, three cities, claiming lack of resources to comply with the housing guidelines, pulled out of ABAG.)

CHANGING GOVERNMENTAL STRUCTURES AND PATTERNS

Broad Regional Government?

Decades ago, a leading population analyst wondered how the fragmentation of local government could handle enormous webs of urbanization that were the United States's future. He advised that the best way to deal with urban regions that were politically fragmented, socially atomized, and economically complex would be broad regional government.

In the intervening years, broad regional government has often been viewed as a rational response to governmental fragmentation. And it has been adopted by some cities globally, notably Barcelona, Spain.

But regional government has not been politically acceptable in the United States. Indeed, even regional agencies for one function—say, public transit—can be suspect. Anyone who thinks politicians in Oakland, San Francisco, and the surrounding suburban cities will agree to unify the Bay Area's competing transit systems, for example, is under the influence of a legal or illegal substance.

Is small, fragmented government, and a great deal of it, more or less democratic than other options? Here, ideology determines one's views. Neoconservatives assume that small governments are more responsive to citizens' preferences than big, bureaucratic ones. Thus, they prefer fragmentation to centralized governments. Others hold diametrically opposed views. Some years ago political scientist Gregory R. Weiher (1991:195), one dissenting voice, wrote that fragmented local government is *anti*democratic: "The American model of democracy," Weiher wrote, "requires a citizenry in which social groups are not radically isolated from one another"; but "the system of urban jurisdictional boundaries" sponsors segregation of many kinds: "whites from blacks, lower income groups from the middle class, religious groups from one another." Thus, in his view, fragmentation is an instrument of antidemocracy.

There are some strong regional agencies in the United States as well as regional land-use planning organizations. There is even one umbrella-type agency that is essentially an areawide planning and coordinating agency: the Metropolitan Council of the Twin Cities, Minneapolis–St. Paul, area. It has a tax-sharing formula whereby the region shares some of the tax revenue from new development. It serves a seven-county metro area, providing some essential services to the region, including the region's largest bus system.

As of the late 2000s however, there is no broad-based regional government in the United States. It has proved to be too hard of a sell politically.

How, then, are—and will—public services be delivered to metropolitan and megalopolitan residents? Probably, mostly by muddling through. Thus far, public services have been provided via a combination of traditional responses, minor adaptations, and innovative experiments. (It is noteworthy that in some areas, typically upscale, some formerly public services have been replaced or supplemented by private guards, private schools, and private police.)

Traditional Responses and Minor Adaptations

On the more traditional side, residents of the urban fringe (unincorporated areas near a municipality that have urban service needs) are getting such urban services as police and fire protection in various ways: (1) by incorporation, thus creating a new municipality; (2) by contracting with the county or a nearby municipality for services; (3) by annexation; and (4) by forming special districts. Each of these techniques has its own problems and prospects.

Incorporation creates yet another local government, thereby adding to local fragmentation. Further, if its county is already financially strapped, the newly incorporated city can deprive the county of needed revenue. Contracting for services allows urban fringe residents to keep their highly valued rural environment, but at whose expense? Some observers feel that under contracting arrangements, city residents pay more than their fair share because residents of unincorporated areas don't pay for large capital investments (jails, fire-houses, etc.) or for training city employees.

The problem of coordinating special districts has already been noted. Recall also that the number of special districts has grown enormously since the 1950s, resulting in even more fragmentation of the metropolis.

Annexation is the only traditional response that doesn't lead to an increased number of local governments. Annexation results in political integration rather than metropolitan government. However, since it requires boundary changes, annexation is not feasible in many MSAs, where most land is already incorporated into municipalities.

To cope with disputes over annexation, incorporation, and special district formation, some states have set up boundary commissions. So far, they have helped somewhat to check the further proliferation of local governments, but they have had little success in reforming the existing crazy quilt of local governments in the metropolis.

Innovative Experiments

In France, Canada, and West Bengal, to take just a few examples, politicians have successfully forged innovations in sub-national governments in recent decades. This has not been the case in the United States. From after World War II until the 1970s, a few scholars and politicians in the United States touted innovative experiments in regional and metropolitan government, but attempts at structural innovation sputtered by the 1990s.

Since 2000, there has been almost none in the United States (the exception: Louisville's consolidation with suburban Jefferson County in 2000). Further, scholarly as well as citizen interest in structural changes at the local and regional levels of government became like the Spice Girls, grunge, and fluorescent T-shirts: out of style.

In the United States, the most ambitious proposals—broad regional government and a single, unified metropolitan government (called a "one-tier" or "one-level" government)—remain mere plans on a drawing board. But in North America, there are four models of structural change currently in operation plus one entrepreneurial framework for delivering public services.

Metro: To date, the most ambitious effort at structural change in North America is the metropolitan government of Toronto, Canada. Metropolitan Toronto first established a "two-tier" **federation** in 1953; Metro operated until 1997 when it was again transformed.

The original Metro consisted of a single, areawide government as the first tier and the preexisting local governments as the second tier. The newly created metropolitanwide first tier, called the Municipality of Metropolitan Toronto (or Metro), was governed by representatives from the preexisting governments: Toronto's municipal government plus 12 suburban governments. Metro had jurisdiction over the entire metropolitan area. It had power over many important urban functions: property assessment, water supply, sewage disposal, mass transit, health services, welfare, administration of justice, arterial roads, parks, public housing, redevelopment, and planning.

Under Toronto's two-tier plan, some functions were retained by local governments while others were shared with Metro. For instance, Metro maintained reservoirs and pumping stations, but the second tier of local governments handled the distribution of water to their residents. By the 1990s, the population of the Greater Toronto area had grown enormously, and the area had become, according to the United Nations, "the most multicultural city [*sic*] in the world" (in MOST Clearing House, n.d.).

By the end of the twentieth century, many believed that Metro had become irrelevant because it no longer covered most of the population in the ever-growing urban area. (In 2005, the Greater Toronto area had a population of about 5.8 million residents.) After a referendum, which failed to win voter support in all six municipalities involved, an amalgamation was pushed through by the ruling Ontario political party. Thus, in 1998 Metro morphed into a regional municipality formed of smaller municipalities. The larger Metro government was retained, and the existing city of Toronto and five other smaller municipalities became a new city of Toronto.

Note that a Toronto-like framework was adapted in Montreal, Canada, in 2002. However, many suburbanites, particularly English-speaking and rich ones, protested the annexations of their suburbs into the proposed federated system; they viewed a federation as a power grab by larger cities, particularly French-identified Montreal. The Montreal Urban Community was transformed into a federated system, but as of 2006, 32 out of the 89 constituent communities voted to "demerge" or de-amalgamate.

The comprehensive urban county: Short of federation or amalgamation, there is another model of structural change: the comprehensive urban county plan. Operating in Miami-Dade County, Florida, since 1957, a two-tier government gives the county government a powerful and integrating role over an area of 2,054 square miles and 27 municipalities.

Among its functions, the comprehensive urban county government (Figure 4.4) is authorized to promote the entire area's economy, own and operate mass-transit systems, construct express-ways, provide uniform health and welfare services, and maintain central records and communication for fire and police protection.

Consolidation: City–county consolidation is another technique. It is a one-government, not a two-tier, approach.

Usually, this type of governmental reorganization consists of the total or substantial merging of the county government with the largest city (or all municipalities) within its boundaries. From World War II to the 1990s, there were four major city–county consolidations, three of which remain: Jacksonville–Duval County, Florida (1967), which in 1992 became a *former* consolidation; Baton Rouge-East Baton Rouge Parish (the parish is

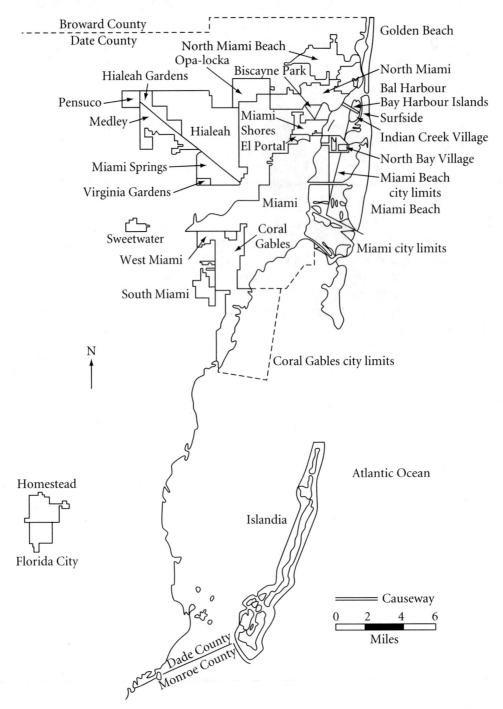

FIG. 4.4 | *METROPOLITAN MIAMI-DADE COUNTY, FLORIDA. In its early years, the metropolitan government in Miami-Dade County (formerly Dade County), faced opposition and a continuing struggle between the county and municipalities, the two levels of government that composed it. Later, however, residents turned their attention from government structure to less abstract issues, such as racial and ethnic tension, changing demographics, hurricane disaster relief, high crime rates, and poverty. By 2005, poverty rates had remained essentially unchanged since 1979 (although the county's population doubled between 1960 and 1990). Those affected disproportionately by high poverty rates as of 2007 were Hispanics, the majority group in the county (61 percent of the total population with about 17 percent living in poverty), and African Americans, with about 29 percent below the poverty line (Miami-Dade county's Planning and Zoning Department, 2007, http://www.co.miami-dade.fl.us/planzone/pdf/Overview%20of%20the%20Socio-Economic.pdf). Also by 2007, Miami-Dade's county manager presided over 30,000 employees, 60 departments serving over 2.3 million residents, and a budget of $6.9 billion.*

Louisiana's equivalent of the county) in 1947; Nashville-Davidson County, Tennessee (1962); and Indianapolis-Marion County, Indiana (1969).

In the 1990s, two Georgia city–county consolidations took place: Athens-Clarke County and Augusta-Richmond County.

Special districts: A more moderate type of institutional change is the formation of metropolitanwide special districts, either single- or multipurpose in nature. The former owner of the long-gone World Trade Center in New York City, the Port Authority of New York and New Jersey, is such a special district, one that crosses state as well as municipal boundaries.

Privatization of Public Services

The U.S. government's contracting out to private firms is neither new nor experimental. Wells Fargo Bank horseback riders, known as the Pony Express, delivered the mail west of the Mississippi on contract to the U.S. government. Later, starting in World War II, millions of private employees worked in defense-connected industries on government contracts.

More recently, private soldiers working for contractor Blackwater (better known for assignments in war zones such as Iraq) patrolled post-Katrina streets in New Orleans (Scahill, 2007). (Some claim that the U.S. government "outsources" intelligence work to private contractors, including Lockheed Martin and General Dynamics. They estimate that between 50 and 70 percent of U.S. intelligence work, training, and technology are handled by private firms, making it a sector of at least $20 billion [Chaterjee in Sunnucks, 2007; Shorrock, 2008a]).

What is new at the local level is the growth and range of privatization (also called "privatism"). In the Reagan era, many U.S. communities faced tax revolts, cutbacks in federal funds, shrinking tax collections due to economic recession, and fiscal austerity with continuing demands for services—all at the same time! Localities turned to "entrepreneurial government" as a way to meet the challenges. Local governments contracted with private firms for services or entered partnerships with businesses. At least 75 communities in 15 states, mainly new suburbs and cities hard pressed for revenue, contracted with private companies to provide protection against fire.

Contracting out to private companies or nonprofit organizations became widespread in many U.S. cities.

The range includes Philadelphia's operation of golf courses, homeless shelters, and parking enforcement to private enterprises in Phoenix, Arizona, running building and grounds maintenance, landfill operations, the bus system, garbage collection, and street maintenance. Other cities sold museums to private businesses under leaseback arrangements or contracted out the running of jails and prisons.

The story of Ecorse, Michigan, is instructive. In the 1950s, this small industrial town downriver from Detroit boomed. By the early 1980s, plant closings around Detroit plus cutbacks threatened to nearly sink Ecorse. Indeed, Ecorse became the first U.S. city to go into receivership. The court told an expert on city finance to close Ecorse's gap between revenue and expenditures. What the expert did was to privatize. He contracted out garbage pickups, public works, animal control, and other services. From 1986 to 1991, the $6-million city deficit had been turned into a $100,000 surplus.

Privatization boosters in the United States included Bill Clinton when he was president and many so-called New Democrats. This suggests that in less than a generation people in the United States had changed their expectations of government. In 1968, Robert Kennedy ran for president on a liberal platform, arguing that government was an instrument for the public good. By 1992, the three major candidates for president—Republican, Democrat, and United We Stand—seemed to share the belief that government was the enemy. Even in recent years, U.S. presidential candidates (including sitting senators) have run campaigns as "outsiders" or platforms vowing to "change Washington."

Candidates' running away from identification with government coincided with calls to "reinvent government" and to privatize public services. One best-selling book, *Reinventing Government* (1992), had great impact.

(Some, including Shorrock [2008b], claim that Vice President Al Gore was particularly taken with the efficiency claims of privatization.) Written by privatization's leading U.S. advocate, David Osborne, and his coauthor Ted Gaebler, a former city manager in California, it argued that local government bureaucracy had outlived its mission (to fight corruption) and usefulness. Their fix: more market-oriented government to meet declining revenues and increasing demands for consumer services. Subsequently, Osborne and Peter Plastrik offered strategies for *Banishing Bureaucracy* (1998) and suggested tools for transforming government (2001).

The Report Card

Have these innovations been success stories or not? Opinions differ widely. Most observers think that Toronto's two-tier government has made substantial strides toward rational policymaking for the metropolis.

Comprehensive urban counties: Scholars give only a C or C+ to Miami-Dade County's comprehensive urban county plan. One assessment points to considerable instability in the relationship between the urban county government and preexisting municipal governments, as well as continuing fiscal and administrative problems. And some say that the Miami-Dade County's two-tier arrangement suffered from continuing rivalry between the county and cities for the allegiance and control of their citizenry. Meanwhile, government structure is not a burning issue for Miami-Dade residents; they are more interested in less abstract issues such as jobs, crime, and racial–ethnic tension.

Consolidations: City–county consolidations face great opposition usually from outlying residents who must approve the consolidation by popular vote. But sometimes opposition comes from central city residents (who also must approve the change).

Special districts: As for the most moderate structural reform, the metropolitanwide special district, it has made significant gains in dealing with pressing metropolitan needs but is limited to one or a few functions. Further, like special districts that are not metropolitanwide, it is criticized for its nonaccountability to the people it serves.

Privatization: Privatization has vocal supporters and detractors. Boosters praise its cost savings, efficiency, and accountability. Libertarians tend to be its biggest cheerleader. Osborne and Plastrik (1998) claim that Indianapolis saved more than $1 million over 7 years by privatizing. Detractors disagree for a host of reasons. Neoconservative thinkers don't want to *re*invent government; they want to *dis*invent government—at least until recently, they said they did. Some wanted less bureaucracy, which meant less government. But some liberal critics call contracting out a union-busting strategy designed to weaken or destroy public employee unions by wringing concessions from them. Further, they note, governments are a major employer of so-called minorities; reducing government jobs has a disproportionately negative impact on people of color and women. Others fear that if public schools and prisons are turned over to for-profit agencies, there will be less accountability to all citizens or, they warn, private prisons and private jails threaten civil rights, leaving prisoners with less protection against brutality and arbitrary discipline and not guaranteeing "customers" the rights of citizens.

Other criticisms of privatization abound. One concerns the privatized services' ability to serve everyone equally. For example, they claim that private fire departments left nonsubscribers' homes burning while fighting fires at subscribers' homes. Meantime, some critics warn of opportunities for a new kind of bossism; they fear that the contract bidding process could degenerate into patronage in pinstripes.

Finally, radical scholars and activists wonder who wins the most under privatization. Some think that the profit motive may be a powerful incentive but ill-suited to achieving public-policy objectives because the payoffs serve narrow, private interests. Sometime ago, Harvard scholar Elaine Bernard (1993) offered a more blistering critique, saying that privatism is part of a conscious effort by business to decrease public expectations of government and thereby limit more progressive options.

To conclude: It appears that the current crazy quilt of local government is being patched up with bits and pieces. There is no whole new cloth.

Why have efforts to reform local government structure met with so little success? First, many interest groups correctly perceive that major structural changes would not be in their narrowly defined self-interest. Suburbanites, for example, tend to oppose any reform that links their future to the fiscal and political problems of their nearby city. African American and Latino leaders in big cities often oppose metropolitanwide government because they could lose their recently won power in some central cities. Northern Democrats tend to resist metropolitanwide government if Republicans form a numerical majority in the metro area as a whole but not in the central city.

Second, structural reform is hard to sell to voters. By contrast, metropolitanwide special districts can be established either without a popular vote or by state law requiring a popular majority in the entire area. Federation, comprehensive urban counties, and city–county consolidations usually require popular majorities in all of the municipalities involved, a very difficult consensus to obtain.

Scholars don't agree on how metropolitan politics should be structured. One group, the centralists or consolidationists, claims that there are too many local governmental units to provide efficient, effective, and responsible government. Their solutions: centralized metropolitan or even broad regional government. Another group holds that government is not decentralized enough to provide responsive government. Their solutions: community control or neighborhood government. Finally, still another group thinks that the present system works well and is highly desirable because it allows citizens to maximize their choices in the consumption of public goods (e.g., through choice in housing location). This group has no proposed solutions because it doesn't define fragmentation as a problem.

Whatever scholars propose about metropolitan politics, citizens dispose in the end. Proposed reforms of any sort inspire yawns or fear—fear of more bureaucracy, more expense, less control, or changes in the balance of local power. And yawns because the connections between structure and policy outcomes, too often, remain unexplained or seemingly too boring for citizens to care about. Thus, the chances of reshaping U.S. local government seem dim.

THE FEDERAL ROLE IN URBAN AFFAIRS

Even without structural reorganization, local government priorities and programs in the United States have changed dramatically since the New Deal in the 1930s. Corporate business decisions have had significant impacts on localities, such as where to locate a new office or where to invest or disinvest.

Here, let's focus on another important external agent of change: the federal government. Federal officials have pushed (critics say forced) cities to rethink their programs with a variety of incentives, penalties, and mandated duties.

We now turn to a brief history of federal expansion in local life. It is divided into three eras: 1930s–1950s, 1960s–1992, and 1992–summer 2008.

Expansion of Federal Involvement in U.S. Life, 1930s–1950s

Since the 1930s, the federal government has been playing a larger role in U.S. life. The expansion of federal involvement in the economic and social life of the country has significantly affected metropolitan politics, both directly and indirectly. This means that the question "Who runs this town?" can't be answered without reference to the federal government.

It was during the Great Depression of the 1930s that the role of the federal government in U.S. life began to grow. Amid the bread lines and competing ideologies of the time (ranging from radical proposals to redistribute wealth and power, technocratic manifestos to let scientists and engineers run government, and hate campaigns blaming African Americans and Jews for economic distress to demagogic appeals for fascist-type rule), President Franklin D. Roosevelt's New Deal administration moved decisively to maintain social order and economic security. (Radical critics say that it worked to *save* capitalism; conservative critics, to *end* capitalism.) Millions of people in the United States, assumed to be "temporarily poor" during the Depression, were provided some form of social security through New Deal programs. Many functions once handled privately (by family, charities, etc.) or not at all were assumed by the federal government.

According to urban historian Richard C. Wade, the growth of federal power under the New Deal "developed out of the intractability of 25 percent unemployment, a stagnating economy and the desperation of millions" (1982:21). New Deal programs did not take over state and local rights: "Those governments simply had no capacity to meet even the most immediate relief needs, much less to plan for the future." The New Deal added programs that provided a safety net, such as a minimum wage, unemployment insurance, and Social Security. It also offered major assistance to middle-class citizens via such programs as the Federal Housing Administration's below-market-rate mortgages and the Federal Deposit Insurance Corporation, guaranteeing some bank savings.

Subsequently, during World War II and after, the role of the federal government kept growing. (As might be predicted, so did the role of private interests that sought some of the growing state's resources.) Most citizens accepted the centralized system in Washington, D.C., and new programs served new needs, such as the GI Bill of Rights for returning service personnel.

Meanwhile, the "temporarily poor" didn't disappear, and the national interest of a world power was translated into the need for defense industries located throughout the country and efficient transport links. Soon federal funds flowed into and around the nation's small towns as well as big cities. At the same time, modern technology and corporate business organization expanded significantly, and the Springdales of the nation—small towns and hamlets—found themselves in the midst of a mass society (Vidich and Bensman, [1958] 1968). As a result, decisions made in faraway federal agencies and corporate headquarters affected the lives of Americans in cities and rural areas, whether they realized it or not.

Federal policies don't have to be labeled "urban" to affect urban life. Indeed, many federal programs not so designated have changed the fabric of the metropolis as much as, or more than, funds earmarked for cities. Let's take a look at two such post-World War II programs: housing and transportation.

How Federal Policy Affected Postwar Housing and Transportation

Housing

Beginning with the New Deal, the U.S. federal government has pursued policies intended to strengthen financial institutions that provide mortgage money for housing, particularly single-family, detached houses. For instance, the Federal Housing Administration (FHA) was created in the midst of the Depression, when millions of homeowners were defaulting on mortgage payments because they were out of work, housing construction was at a virtual standstill, and banks were going bankrupt. The FHA was established to provide mortgage insurance to protect lenders (banks) against the risk of default on long-term, low-down-payment mortgage loans. The FHA contributed to a gradual recovery of the home finance industry during the 1930s, and then it spurred the massive post-World War II suburban housing boom.

Other federal housing credit institutions in the United States (e.g., the Federal National Mortgage Association, popularly called Fannie Mae) helped to create a national secondary mortgage market so that housing construction funds could flow freely into growth areas. (Since then, a private market for poor credit risks developed: the so-called subprime mortgage sector. "Subprime" borrowers are less than creditworthy risks.) Most blame failures in the housing sector—at least to a significant degree—for the faltering of the U.S. economy in 2007 and beyond. (It is noteworthy that the Republican George W. Bush administration—led by Secretary of the Treasury Hank Paulson, one-time head of a major Wall Street securities firm—sponsored financial aid to Fannie Mae and Freddie Mac, another big, government-sponsored housing credit institution, in 2008.)

What impact did these post-World War II federal housing policies have on cities and suburbs? An enormous impact. By stimulating suburban growth, federal programs underwrote the exodus of white middle-class residents from central cities. In so doing, they helped to cement metropolitanwide housing patterns of economic and racial segregation.

Transportation

Similarly, the billions of dollars poured into highway construction by Congress after World War II had a broad impact on the metropolis. The new interstate highway system, funded 90 percent with federal money, allowed commercial and industrial enterprises to move out of their central city locations and relocate in the suburbs. These location decisions by private business contributed to the erosion of the central city's tax base and to its financial stagnation.

To conclude: Whether intended or not, national policies—not specifically deemed urban—have helped to change the shape and character of U.S. cities since World War II. In particular, federal policies opened up the suburbs, spurred regional growth in Sunbelt cities where new defense-related industries were generously supported, and provided the infrastructure (roads, airports) for private business to serve a national and global mass market. Cities, legal creatures of the state, increasingly became economically and socially tied to the national and international political economy.

From Federalism to the New Federalism, 1960s–1992

In the 1960s, the number of federal programs aimed specifically at the metropolis rose dramatically. So did funding levels. Not surprisingly, the size and number of federal agencies that implement urban-oriented programs followed suit.

A cabinet-level agency, the Department of Housing and Urban Development (HUD), was established by President Lyndon B. Johnson in 1965 specifically to address urban needs. A year later, the Department of Transportation (DOT) was set up, increasing the national government's already-active role in financing urban transit. Other cabinet-level departments expanded their urban programs as part of LBJ's Great Society. New programs, including the controversial War on Poverty, channeled funds directly to cities or urban community groups.

Those were the heady days of Head Start, Job Corps, Model Cities, Foster Grandparents, Legal Services, Community Action, and so on. To liberals, these 1960s Great-Society programs represented a step in the right direction: government intervention to provide equal opportunity for all citizens. To radicals, these programs represented government's attempt to keep cities calm and co-opt the poor by throwing out a few crumbs instead of attacking the capitalist structures that put people in poverty. To conservatives, these programs represented "a ragbag."

When President Richard M. Nixon started his second term in 1972, he proposed a New Federalism. He promised to take powers away from the federal government and give authority and flexibility to the state and local governments. The showpiece of Nixon's New Federalism was **general revenue sharing**, a program with few strings attached. Funds could be used to finance nearly any local government program. (Before the 15-year revenue-sharing program ended in 1987, $85 billion was distributed to 39,000 cities and towns, where the money was spent to purchase a variety of products and services, from flowers to fire trucks.)

President Nixon and his successor, the late Gerald Ford, did not destroy LBJ's Great Society, but they did change its course. While keeping up the level of federal spending for local programs, they redirected funds away from big cities in the Northeast, considered Democratic strongholds, to the urban South and West.

The numbers tell the story of federal expansion. In one decade, 1969–1979, federal outlays to state and local governments quadrupled to $85 billion, much of it being spent in cities (U.S. Office of Management and Budget, 1978:175). In percentage terms, cities' dependence on federal aid for their general revenue grew from 4 percent to 14 percent from 1965 to 1980.

Then, the Reagan–George H. W. Bush "revolution" changed all that. President Ronald Reagan introduced his New Federalism in his 1981 State of the Union message. Underpinned by the conservative/libertarian ideas of Milton Friedman, Reagan's New Federalism decentralized many federal activities to states and local governments, assuring that such decentralized programs would be more responsive to the two most interested groups: the people they were meant to help and the people who were paying for them.

New Tasks, Less Money

However, instead of sustaining the level of federal funds flowing to states and cities, the Reagan and George H. W. Bush administrations slashed the funding of federally-financed, locally-administered programs. Many federal grants-in-aid for education, public works, mass transit, and housing were cut or cut out. From 1980 to 1992, federal dollars spent on U.S. cities declined by 59 percent. Briefly put, the federal government gave the states new tasks but less money.

Cutbacks in federal aid were accompanied by stagflation, high interest rates, and bad economic times. This combination of hard times and budget cuts left localities tax-starved and defunded. Which is what many conservatives wanted: Governments could do less with less money.

More than half of the state and city governments in the United States faced serious financial shortfalls by 1990. Liberals complained. Urbanist George Sternlieb of Rutgers University opined, "We don't have New Federalism, we have New Feudalism, where every community fends for itself with a hodgepodge of responsibilities and taxing powers" (in Hinds and Eckholm, 1990:All). Worst-case budget scenarios became common. For example, hundreds of patients and doctors jammed into San Francisco's City Hall to complain that more cuts to health clinics would endanger lives. The next day, hundreds of children and parents went to City Hall to complain that more library cuts would endanger the literacy of the next generation. Competition for scarce funds between libraries and health clinics was so fierce that one advocate for health care drove home his cause like this: "Dead people can't read books" (in Sandalow, 1993:1).

Severe cutting, even gutting, of cities' social programs raised critical voices to a fever pitch. Reporter Bob Scheer called local government the "garbage can of American politics," left to pick up the pieces of "problems (e.g., crime, drugs, disoriented vets) that the federal and state governments have failed to adequately deal with" while "their tax base is pared to the bone" (1993:1).

To conclude: Starting with the New Deal, the federal government became heavily involved in a wide range of urban programs, from child nutrition and law enforcement to community development. Cities lobby Congress intensely for programs through both nationwide organizations and individual lobbyists.

Long ago, political scientist John Mollenkopf (1983) pointed out that which political party controls Congress does make a difference to cities. In his study of urban legislation from 1933 to 1980, Mollenkopf argued that when Republicans had national control, they redirected money away from central cities to the suburbs and newer metropolitan areas of the Sunbelt. Further, Republicans restructured intergovernmental aid—by channeling it through states and block grants, for instance—to ensure that voters in central cities had the least possible influence.

The balance between city and suburban political power started shifting mightily to the suburbs in 1972 with Nixon's general revenue sharing. By 1992, more than one-half of U.S. cities were saddled with major service burdens and limited options. In a time of economic decline, they faced decreased federal and state aid, state prohibitions against raising local taxes, and widespread suburban antiurbanism.

From 1992 to summer 2008, no major presidential candidate specifically addressed urban issues such as crushing service burdens or homelessness. This neglect would not have surprised urban historian Richard C. Wade. A generation earlier, he noted that the country's political and social power had been permanently reallocated, completing the "suburban captivity of American politics" (1982:21). Of course, Wade could not see the future except through a glass darkly. He did not predict that, by 2005, the percentage of poor in many suburbs around the largest U.S. cities would outnumber the percentage of poor inside central cities. Neither did Wade foresee that the rising cost of energy might push some suburbanites back to U.S. cities, thus changing the urban-suburban mix in the United States.

A Nameless Period, 1992–Summer 2008

Unlike previous administrations, neither President Bill Clinton nor President George W. Bush stamped a name, such as the New Federalism, on his urban program. (Some critics, however, called these policies "fend for yourself federalism.") During their tenures, there was no easily identifiable urban policy. Perhaps on purpose. That is, political purpose. Even so, federal programs (or the lack of them) aimed at cities and suburbs continue to have serious impacts.

Clinton's Urban Policies

During the Clinton years (1993–2001), unemployment dropped to record lows. So did inflation. The federal budget was in surplus. Crime rates dropped in many places. These greatly affected cities.

Under Clinton, several policies and laws also had great impacts on cities and cityfolk. For example, Clinton expanded the Earned Income Tax Credit (EITC), which proved to be the Clinton's most effective antipoverty measure; it provided the working poor with more income than any other program. Further, Clinton's Department of Housing and Urban Development promoted community development corporations as a way to revitalize poor urban neighborhoods; in Los Angeles (and other cities), community development corporations built most of the affordable housing that was added to the city's inventory in over 10 years.

However, critics hold that Clinton's policies had little to do with improved urban conditions. They argue that cities improved basically because of an unprecedented national economic expansion. Others think that this economic expansion was reinforced by federal policies sponsored by Clinton, particularly those that reduced joblessness.

Clinton's most controversial urban-oriented legislation was the welfare reform bill of 1996: the Personal Responsibility and Work Opportunity Reconciliation Act (PRWORA). The day it passed in August 1996, Clinton announced that PRWORA would end welfare "as we know it." The day after, *a Washington Post* reporter hailed Clinton's bill as "historic," rewriting 60 years of social policy, "ending the federal guarantee of cash assistance to the poor and turning welfare programs over to the states" (Vobedja, 1996). The bill required recipients to work (so-called workfare rather than welfare) and limited benefits to 5 years.

Clinton's PRWORA was intensely disliked in many quarters, particularly by noncentrist Democrats. Some believed it pulled the "safety net" out from under the nation's least fortunate. Others dubbed it "forced labor," not "workfare" (e.g., Dunlea, 1997). The National Organization of Women called it "punitive" (Lee and Weinstein, 1996). But by spring 2007 no one in the mainstream media or in national politics seemed to care one way or the other.

George W. Bush's Urban Policies

During George W. Bush's presidency, the focus shifted. Bush preferred private answers to public challenges. Thus, he favored cutting taxes, particularly for those at the top of the income ladder; reducing government regulations on business; and privatizing previously government-funded public services such as drug counseling. These measures were aimed, his administration said, at increasing investment and jobs and saving taxpayers' dollars. Conservatives and libertarians were pleased with such measures, assumed to stimulate the economy and promote the "trickle-down" effect. (The other major Bush initiative in terms of funding—U.S. military spending for wars in Iraq and Afghanistan—did not get widespread support from libertarians.)

A U.S. economic recession ended in late 2001. But the recovery over the following 2 years was mainly jobless as U.S. firms shipped white- and blue-collar jobs overseas. Thus, during Bush's first 3 years as president, unemployment *increased* (from 4 to 6 percent). Between 2000 and 2003, median household income fell, and the poverty rate rose (from 11.3 percent to 12.5 percent or, otherwise put, from 31.1 million to 35.9 million). After 9/11, funds for a domestic "war on terrorism," together with big tax cuts for some and big military spending, led to spiraling budget deficits. Discretionary funds for social or antipoverty programs dried up, which is what many conservatives thought prudent. Later during his administration, bank bailouts and credit infusions into the banking system—designed to stem financial crises that began in 2007—would increase the deficit more.

Critics say that the Bush administration's "war on terrorism" and "homeland security" programs have had a disproportionate and negative impact on U.S. cities. They claim that the federal government has required cities to dramatically increase security (e.g., at airports, ports, and sporting events) and to improve emergency preparations but that the cities were not given adequate funds to pay for these programs. According to sociologist Peter Dreier (2004), cities were spending $70 million a week out of their own coffers just to comply with each "orange alert" security threat from the federal Department of Homeland Security. Similarly, others argue that cities were asked to comply with expensive federal mandates, especially homeland security and antiterrorism initiatives, but that federal funds were not provided to help pay for the mandated programs.

Aside from responses to financial crises, such as federal intervention in the banking and credit markets, two Bush initiatives have had the most impact on metro areas. They are the following: (1) No Child Left Behind and (2) Faith-Based Initiatives.

No Child Left Behind

The No Child Left Behind Act of 2001 requires local schools to raise standards via testing and to issue annual report cards on students' improvements. The bill requires federal and state governments to punish schools that don't meet the standards. Critics say that Bush failed to ask for enough funds that could pay for hiring more teachers, reducing class sizes, and improving facilities that could help low-achieving students, especially students in inner-city schools. They also claim that there is a mismatch: Needy inner-city schools may be the most likely to lack the resources and funds to comply with the act and thrive.

Critics also point out that there may be widespread cheating in the program to obtain better results. Teachers at 123 schools in California, for example, admitted to helping students cheat on exams given to meet the requirements of No Child Left Behind. According to *San Francisco Chronicle* reporters, "Incentives to bend the rules are strong in the No Child Left Behind era, when persistently low scores can shut down a school, trigger a takeover or force teacher transfers, experts say" (Asimov et al., 2007:A1).

Faith-Based Initiatives

Under President Bush, Congress increased funds to private religious organizations to provide social services such as prisoner reentry programs, drug counseling, homeless shelters, and food banks. How was this done? In part by "earmarks." A *New York Times* analysis (in Henriques and Lehren, 2007:A7) observes that the number of earmarks (narrowly-tailored appropriations that bypass the normal appropriations and competitive bidding processes) increased sharply in recent years: From 1989 to January 2007, Congress approved about 900 earmarks to religious groups, totaling $318 million. In comparison, fewer than 60 earmarks for faith-based groups were passed in the 1997–1998 congressional session.

Aside from earmarks, Bush bypassed Congress and operated instead through executive orders and regulatory changes at the cabinet level to insure faith-based programs. In 2002, Bush created the Faith-Based and Community Initiative (WHOFBCI) in the White House, which, according to its press release (White House, 2006), awarded more than $2.1 million in grants to religious organizations in fiscal year 2005 by seven federal agencies. Again bypassing Congress, in 2006 Bush created, by executive order, the Center for Faith-Based and Community Initiatives at the U.S. Department of Homeland Security. The center is charged with coordinating Homeland Security's efforts to remove obstacles to faith-based and community organizations in providing disaster relief services.

Typically, faith-based initiatives are popular with groups considered part of the base of the Republican Party, including evangelical Christians. Many others question their constitutionality and/or their effectiveness.

Others question the use of executive orders and other devices to bypass Congress. Indeed, some called him an imperial president.

To conclude: During Clinton's presidency, the U.S. economy surged, a not-unimportant factor in promoting more jobs and more livable cities. During this strong economy, Clinton fulfilled his promise as a centrist Democrat, getting a welfare-reform bill passed (that enraged "progressives" and those called "leftists" by those who weren't).

Later, George W. Bush ran for U.S. president as a "compassionate conservative." Whether his administrations lived up to the compassionate part is a matter of great dispute. However, most agree that his nonfiscal policies (not his second administration's bailouts of private firms, for example, part of his fiscal policy) were more conservative than those of any other administration in living memory.

With what some call "fend for yourself federalism" (Morgan et al., 2006) under Bush, federally funded urban programs were slashed, thanks to a combination of factors, including ideology (a preference for privatization, including faith-based social programs and its view of poverty as being due primarily to personal character flaws), war spending, a budget deficit, tax cuts of about $1.3 trillion, and perhaps politics: Gore beat Bush among urban voters, and two groups long defined as urban voters—African Americans and Hispanics—did not vote overwhelmingly for Bush.

THE QUESTION RECONSIDERED: WHO RUNS THIS TOWN?

Federal regulations, state laws, areawide planning suggestions, special-district decisions, county legislation, neighborhood requests. This list suggests that cities are not masters of their own fate. Instead, they are just one layer of government operating within a web of government—some call it a marble cake—of overlapping and intersecting layers.

To attain one's political goals, knowledge of the formal structures of government is essential. Knowing who's in charge in this governmental maze—who to blame, where to go for an authorization, where to protest a decision—is the first step in getting something done in city politics.

Here is a case study of one citizens' group, Bananas, that successfully worked its way through the maze of political structures. It highlights the necessity of appreciating the complexities of government's formal organization. It also shows that, in the United States, any meaningful response to the question "Who runs this town?" must take into account the web of government reaching from Washington, D.C. (and beyond), to the neighborhood day-care center.

Case Study: What Bananas Learned About the Formal Structure Of Government

The sign over a small building in north Oakland, California, reads BANANAS. No fruit is for sale there. Instead, on the front porch lie ice-cream containers, fabric remnants, and wood scraps—all ingredients for children's play projects.

Inside the building, organized chaos prevails. A dozen women are answering phones and giving information about day care as actively as stockbrokers tell their clients about hot prospects. Parents and children stream into and out of the information area. A social service worker answers the "Warm Line," a pre—crisis counseling service for parents with day-care needs.

What's going on here? The name says it all: Bananas, a multipurpose community service, helps to prevent parents from "going bananas" by providing various kinds of assistance with their preschool children. It does all this in 11 languages, including English, Mien, Thai, and French.

Bananas didn't happen overnight. It grew out of years of frustration, organizing, and political struggle. The program director had gained some prior political experience during her fight to organize an employees' union on the University of California at Berkeley campus. Staff members learned by personal experience. Their first lesson was how to deal with and through governmental structures. To a significant degree, Bananas exists today because it learned this lesson.

In 1972, a small group of women—Bananas—became concerned that Berkeley had no place where parents could get information to help to set up play groups for preschool children. (Later, the group moved to nearby north Oakland; Bananas now serves the northern part of its county, Alameda.) This nonhierarchical group had no money or community support, but the members did have energy and commitment to their cause. They began to organize information assistance to parents, children, and day-care providers. After 4 years of hard work, they began to deal with city officials, trying to get government support for their activities.

In the process, they discovered whom to approach ("know-who") to get their project moving. Here are some of the lessons they learned.

1. *Find out who makes the decisions in city government.* Berkeley has a council-manager form of government. The city manager has the final word under this system, and negotiations for funding were carried out directly with him. Bananas didn't deal with the mayor. The specific budget recommendation came from the city manager since his office prepares the city budget.

2. *Find out what the city is authorized to fund.* There is no prohibition in Berkeley against using tax-payers' money for day-care activities. If there were, Bananas would have had to seek funding elsewhere.

3. *Find out what government agencies have an interest in the activity (and how they relate to city government).* Berkeley, like other towns, exists in a web of governments. Bananas had to learn the structure regarding child care. At the level closest to home is the Berkeley Unified School District, a special district run by an elected school board. The board, which is not accountable to city government, was often in disagreement with city officials. The school district provides child care for preschool children in the schools. Thus, it is an interested party regarding other day-care activities in the community. Bananas dealt with the school board, not the Berkeley City Council, to coordinate information and referral activities.

Bananas also dealt with another interested party: the Berkeley Parks and Recreation Department. This city department administered a voucher system, paying low-income and working mothers a stipend for day care. Bananas' staff members worked with the Parks and Recreation Department on a daily basis to refer voucher recipients to appropriate day-care centers.

Yet another interested party was the county. Alameda County, in which Berkeley is located, operated day care-related programs. The county's Social Services Department administered a federal program giving child-care vouchers to eligible recipients. When Bananas felt that the county was not taking full advantage of the voucher program, they pressed for wider benefits. To accomplish this, they went to the County Board of Supervisors, not the Berkeley City Council.

Bananas also dealt with a state-mandated regional center for child care, a clearinghouse for so-called special-needs children. To provide clear guidance to parents, Bananas had to go to this regional planning organization for information.

Then there was the state of California. It, too, was (and is) involved in child care. (The state subsidizes certain types of day care for children with special needs.) Bananas learned about the direct aid the state could provide to their clients.

Indirectly, through the county programs, Bananas was involved with federal funding. They also found out that the-then Department of Health, Education and Welfare (later divided into two cabinet-level departments, Health and Human Services and Education) provided direct funding to a few special day-care operations.

So, who runs this town? Bananas moved through the governmental maze to find out. At the level of formal structure, they discovered, often the hard way, that power and authority in their area of concern, child care, were shared by different layers of government and several city bureaucracies.

Eventually, Bananas got what they wanted but not before they learned how informal networks of power operate. That is a theme continued in Chapters 14 and 15.

ANOTHER LOOK

U.S. citizens and scholars agree that the role of government at all levels has increased dramatically since the 1930s. They disagree on whether this is desirable, necessary, or inevitable in mass society. (Yet, most think that this trend will likely continue.)

Concerning local government, U.S. traditions favor fragmented authority and power. While many political scientists (particularly liberals) describe the current crazy quilt of local government as "irrational" and "inefficient," voters have not supported major structural change. Particularly in gloomy economic times, voters have turned their attention else where: how to get more (or the same services) for less (taxes)—at the same time. Some hope that contracting out public services will be an answer to the tax crunch, but critics think that privatization is fraught with possibilities for inequity, corruption, and even a new sort of bossism.

Meanwhile, observers wonder if local governments—whatever their structure—matter much in a global society. To public choice theorists (e.g., Tiebout, 1956), locality does remain important because people choose a particular place to live so that they can choose among bundles of services. But others say that people's residential choice is not dictated by such market logic. Further, critics argue that local politics can no longer meet the burdens that citizens place upon it because a series of factors, including the powers of higher levels of government which combine to hem in local governments and render them powerless to manage the quality of community life.

Perhaps. But at the same time there are local officials and ordinary citizens who reject powerlessness. Some practice spirited acts of nonviolent resistance by taking responsibility for their fellow beings and a small piece of the sky. Others, using the rhetoric of populist rebellion, form private armies and stockpile weapons against what they fear or hate: faraway, big government and urbanism as a way of life. Between these two reactions to powerlessness lies a chasm of difference—and direction. In my view, one looks backward to the values of a (real or romanticized) frontier past and the other accepts (for better and worse) the urban present and the global urban future.

Long ago, two social scientists predicted that there would be an enduring battle between these two orientations. In *Small Town in Mass Society* ([1958] 1968), sociologists Arthur J. Vidich and Joseph Bensman observed that some small farmers and rural town dwellers resisted "perhaps irreversible" trends toward *Gesellschaft* values. They cautioned that the defeat of ruralism in the United States could lead to a populist backlash based on rural hostility and defensiveness:

> POPULIST DEMOCRACY [IDENTIFIED WITH GRASSROOTS DEMOCRACY AND "AMERICANISM"] MAY BECOME THE BASIS FOR NEW SOCIAL MOVEMENTS WHICH COULD SUBVERT THE FOUNDATIONS OF THE PRESENT BY HOLDING TO ROMANTICIZED IMAGES OF THE PAST. AN ORGANIZED NATIVISTIC MOVEMENT BASED PARTLY ON A XENOPHOBIC ISOLATIONISM COULD SHELTER. . .DEFENSIVE POPULISTS [AND] A VARIETY OF OTHER GROUPS WHOSE RESENTMENTS ARE LESS CRYSTALLIZED BUT WHICH COULD FIND A FOCUS IN SOME FORM OF NATIVISM.
>
> ([1958] 1968:346)

This populism had its origins in an earlier democratic ideology, but as Vidich and Bensman warned, it could go sour and become nativistic, antidemocratic, and quasi-totalitarian.

If some accommodation is not worked out between populist patriots (and other groups that have become influential since *Small Town in Mass Society* was published, such as religious conservatives and angry, unemployed people) who uphold "traditional" values and modernists who uphold urbane values of heterogeneity, tolerance, and cosmopolitanism, we can predict that power—not authority—will prevail. Perhaps that is why

Vidich and Bensman ended their community study with a plea to avoid a direct confrontation between the opposing orientations.

KEY TERMS

Annexation   The addition of territory to a unit of government. Annexation usually involves a city's adding adjacent land to meet the problems of metropolitan expansion.

Areawide planning organization   See council of governments.

Authority   Power used in such a way that people see it as legitimate.

Charter   The basic law of a local government unit that defines its powers, responsibilities, and organization. State constitutional or statutory provisions specify the conditions under which charters will be granted.

Charter city   A city whose powers are defined by a charter from the state. Contrast: *general-law city*.

City council   The policymaking and, in some instances, administrative board of a city. City councils are typically unicameral bodies.

City manager   A professional administrator, appointed by the city council, in a council–manager form of government.

Commission form of government   A form of city government in which both legislative and executive powers are exercised by commissioners. Not to be confused with a city commission. Features include (1) the concentration of legislative and executive power in a small group of commissioners elected at large on a nonpartisan ballot; (2) the collective responsibility of the commission to pass ordinances and control city finances; (3) the individual responsibility of each commissioner to head a city department; and (4) the selection of a mayor from among the commissioners, effectively reducing that office to one of largely ceremonial functions.

Council-manager form of government   A form of city government in which the city council appoints a professional administrator, the city manager, to act as the chief executive. With variations from city to city, the essentials of this plan are (1) a small council of five or seven members elected at-large on a nonpartisan ballot, with power to make policy and hire and fire the manager; (2) a professionally-trained manager, with authority to hire and fire subordinates, who is responsible to the council for efficient administration of the city; and (3) a mayor chosen separately or from within the council but with no executive functions.

Council of governments (COG)   A voluntary organization of municipalities and counties concerned with areawide problems in a metropolitan area.

County   A major local government subdivision in the United States. Counties may perform a variety of local government functions, including provision of welfare and social services, administration of libraries, and road repair. Counties are typically governed by boards of supervisors or county commissioners. In rural areas, counties usually act as the general-purpose local government. In urban areas, they act as the general-purpose government for unincorporated territory and provide some services to residents of both unincorporated and incorporated areas within them.

Dillon's rule   A rule (not a law) enunciated by Iowa Judge John F. Dillon, a nineteenth-century authority on municipal corporations, stating that a municipal corporation (such as a city) can exercise only those powers expressly granted to it by state law, those necessarily implied by the granted powers, and those essential for the purposes of the organization. If any doubt exists, it is to be resolved against the local unit in favor of the state.

Federation An approach to municipal governmental reorganization that assigns areawide functions to an areawide or metropolitan government and leaves local functions to existing municipalities. Example: Toronto's Metro government.

General-law city A city created pursuant to the general law of the state in which it is located rather than under a charter.

General revenue sharing An approach to the transfer of federal funds to lower levels of government—states and general-purpose local governments. Under general revenue sharing, states and local governments may use federal monies as they decide; there are no strings attached. This contrasts with program-related monies.

Home rule Power vested in a local government, such as a city, to craft or change its charter and manage its own affairs, subject to the state constitution and the general law of the state. Under home rule, state legislative interference in local affairs is limited.

Hyperpluralism The belief of some political scientists that city governments suffer from too many (*hyper*) private groups and public authorities playing the political game, which results in the paralysis of urban policymaking and the consequent bureaucratic takeover of political functions.

Incorporation The formation of a new city from previously unincorporated territory. State law specifies how new cities are to be incorporated.

Mayor The titular head of city government. The degree of a mayor's legal authority varies. In mayor–council governments, there are strong and weak mayors. In council–manager governments, the city manager runs the city's day-to-day affairs.

Mayor-council form of government A form of city government in which the mayor is elected to serve as the executive officer of the city and an elected council serves as the legislative body.

Municipality The U.S. Census Bureau's term for general-purpose units of local government other than counties. Municipalities include cities, towns and townships, and boroughs.

Reapportionment Redrawing of legislative district lines so that representation in elected government bodies is proportional to the actual population. In 1962 the U.S. Supreme Court ruled in *Baker v. Carr* that representation had to be on a one person, one vote basis.

Special district An independent unit of local government established to provide one or more limited functions, such as water. Special districts are usually created to meet problems that transcend local government boundaries or to bypass taxation and debt restrictions imposed upon local units of government by state law.

Urban county (1) A county with responsibility for providing urban services for incorporated or unincorporated areas within its borders; (2) a county where there is a substantial and densely settled population, giving it the character of a city; or (3) a county that meets specific criteria enabling it to receive certain federal funds.

REFERENCES

Applebome, Peter. 1993. "Heedless of scorners, a G-rated Las Vegas booms in the Ozarks." *New York Times* (national edition) (June 1):B1+.

Asimov, Nanette, et al. 2007. "Teachers who cheat: Some help students during standards test—or fix answers later–and California's safeguards may leave more breaches unreported." *San Francisco Chronicle* (May 13):A1.

Associated Press. 2006. "Suburban poverty rising in U.S.: Report: More than 12 million in suburbs considered poor, outnumbers inner-city figures." CBS News (December 7): http://www.cbsnews.com/stories/2006/12/07/national/main2237136.shtml

Bernard, Elaine. 1993. "On creating a new party." Alternative Radio, Boulder, Colo. (April 2).

Berube, Alan, and Elizabeth Kneebone. 2006. "Two steps back: City and suburban poverty trends 1999–2005." Washington, D.C.: Brookings Institution (December): http://www.brookings.edu/metro/pubs/20061205_citysuburban.htm

Bogart, Beth. "Corruption ia in rhe system!: *In These Times* (February 20–26):5.

Capone, Al. n. d. "Al Capone famous quotes." http://www.quotemountain.com/famous_quote_author/al_capone_famous_quotations

Castle, Mike. 2006. "Delaware would benefit from pro-family, suburban agenda." (May): http://www.castle.house.gov/index.php?option=com_content&task=view&id=249

Cyber National International, Ltd. 1997–2003. "Abraham Lincoln." http://www.cybernation.com/victory/quotations/authors/quotes_lincoln_abraham.html

Davis, Mike. 1993. "Who killed L.A.: The war against the cities." *CrossRoads* 32:2–19.

Dillon, John F. 1911. *Commentaries on the Law of Municipal Corporations*, 5th ed., vol. 1, sec. 237. Boston: Little, Brown.

Dreier, Peter. 2004. "Urban neglect: George W. Bush and the cities: The damage done and the struggle ahead." *Shelterforce Online* (September/October, 137): http://www.nhi.org/online/issues/137/urbanneglect.html

Dunlea, Mark. 1997. "'Welfare reform:' Clinton kills safety net." *Synthesis/Regeneration* 12: http://www.greens.org/s-r/12/12–15.html

Edkins, Keith. n.d. What is the structure of UK local government? http://www.gwydir.demon.co.uk/uklocalgov/structure.htm

Feinstein, Dianne. 1988. "Mayors' tips for the new mayor." *San Francisco Chronicle* (January 9):A5.

Henriques, Diana B., and Andrew Lehren. 2007. "Religious groups reap share of federal aid." *San Francisco Chronicle* (May 13):A7.

Hinds, Michael de Courcy, with Erik Eckholm. 1990. "80's leave state and cities in need." *New York Times* (national edition) (December 30):A1+.

James, Frank. 2006. "Congress' suburbanites vow to fight for suburbs." *The Swamp, Chicago Tribune* Washington Bureaublog: http:weblogs.chicagotribune.com/news/politics/blog/2006/05/congress_suburbanites_vow_to_f.html

Kheel, Theodore W. [1969] 1971. "The Port Authority strangles New York." p. 443–449 in David M. Gordon, ed., *Problems in Political Economy: An Urban Perspective*. Lexington, Mass.: Heath.

Lee, Andrea, and Mira Weinstein. 1996. "Clinton veto needed on punitive welfare legislation." *National NOW Times*: http://www.now.org/nnt/01–96/welfare.html

Mollenkopf, John. 1983. *The Contested City*. Princeton, N.J.: Princeton University Press.

Molotch Harvey. 1990. "Urban deals in comparative perspective." p. 175–198 in John R. Logan and Todd Swanstrom, eds., *Beyond the City Limits: Urban Policy and Economic Restructuring in Comparative Perspective*. Philadelphia: Temple University Press.

Morgan, David R., Robert E. England, and John P. Pelissero. 2006. *Managing Urban America*, 6th ed. Washington, D.C.: CQ Press.

MOST Clearing House. n.d. "Best Practices. Metro Toronto's changing communities: Innovative responses." http://www.vcn.bc.ca/citizens-handbook/unesco/most/usa9.html

National League of Cities. n.d. "About cities: Cities 101. "ithttp://www.nlc.org/about_cities/cities_101/154.aspx

Noonan, Erica. 2007. "New year, old ways: Chinese school grows as parents keep traditions alive." *Boston Globe* (February 15): http://www.boston.com/news/local/articles/2007/02/15/new_year_old_ways/

NPR-Kaiser-Kennedy School Poll. 2002. "Attitudes toward government." http: www.npr.org/programs/specials/poll/govt/gov.toplines.pdf

Osborne, David, and Ted Gaebler. 1992. *Reinventing Government: How the Entrepreneurial Spirit Is Transforming the Public Sector*. Reading, Mass.: Addison-Wesley.

Osborne, David, and Peter Plastrik. 2001. *The Reinventor's Fieldbook: Tools for Transforming Your Government*. New York: John Wiley & Sons.

———. 1998. *Banishing Bureaucracy: The Five Strategies for Reinventing Government*. New York: Plume.

Pelissero, John P., and David Fasenfest. 1988. "A typology of suburban economic development policy." Paper delivered at the annual meeting of the American Political Science Association, Boston, MA, September 3–6.

Rasmussen Reports. 2008. "Americans give low marks to U.S. health care, but 69% rate their health insurance good or excellent." (July 7): www.ramussenreports.com/public_content/politics/issues2/articles/americans_give_low_marks_to_u_s_health_care_but_69_rate_their_health_insurance_good_or_excellent

Roberts, Joel. 2002. "Poll: Little faith in big biz." CBS News (July 10): http://www.cbsnews.com/stories/2002/07/10/opinion/polls/main514732.shtml

———. 2007. "Poll: The politics of health care." CBS News (March 1): http://www.cbsnews.com/stories/2007/03/01/opinion.polls/main2528357.shtml

Sandalow, Marc. 1993. S.F.'s $188 million deficit will force tough choices." *San Francisco Chronicle* (May 17):A1.

Sayre, Wallace, and Herbert Kaufman. 1960. *Governing New York City: Politics in the Metropolis*. New York: Russell Sage.

Scahill, Jeremy. 2007. *Blackwater: The Rise of the World's Most Powerful Mercenary Army*. New York: Nation Books.

Scheer, Bob. 1993. "S.F. soaking up nation's troubles." *San Francisco Examiner* (June 27):A1.

Schneider, William. 1992. "The suburban century begins." *Atlantic Monthly* (July):33–44.

Shorrock, Tim. 2008a. *Spies for Hire: The Secret World of Intelligence Outstanding.* New York: Simon & Schuster.

————. 2008b. Interview on NPR's *Fresh Air* with Terry Gross (May 14).

Sunnucks, Mike. 2007. "Fort Huachuca intelligence center draws private contractors." *Business Journal of Phoenix* (November 7): http://www.bizjournals.com/phoenix/stories/2007/11/05/daily27.html

Thousman. 2008. "San Francisco voted #1 U.S. city by Conde Nast Traveler readers for 16th consecutive year." (October): http://www.onlyinsanfrancisco.com/sfnews/?p=73

Tiebout, Charles. 1956. "A pure theory of local expenditures." *Journal of Political Economy* 64:416–424.

U.S. Bureau of Justice. 2009. "Crime characteristics." (April 21): http://www.ojp.usdoj.gov/bjs/cvict_c.htm

U.S. Bureau of the Census. 2002. 2002 Census of governments. GC01–1P: http://ftp2.census.gov/govs/cog/2002COGprelim_report.pdf

U.S. Office of Management and Budget. 1978. *Special Analyses of the Budget of the United States Fiscal Year* 1979. Washington, D.C.: Government Printing Office.

U.S. Senate. 1966–1967. *Federal Role in Urban Affairs.* Hearings before the Subcommittee on Executive Reorganization of the Committee on Governmental Operations, 89th and 90th Cong., 2nd sess.

Vidich, Arthur J., and Joseph Bensman. [1958] 1968. *Small Town in Mass Society: Class, Power and Religion in a Rural Community.* Princeton, N.J.: Princeton University Press.

Vobedja, Barbara. 1996. "Clinton signs welfare reform, turns programs over to states." *The Tech* 116(31): http://www-tech.mit.edu/V116/N31/clinton.31w.html

Wade, Richard C. 1982. "The suburban roots of the new federalism." *New York Times Magazine* (August 1):20+.

Weiher, Gregory R. 1991. *The Fractured Metropolis: Political Fragmentation and Metropolitan Segregation.* Albany: State University of New York Press.

Weiss, Michael J. 1988. *The Clustering of American.* New York: Harper & Row.

White House. 2006. "WHOFBCI accomplishments in 2006." http://www.whitehouse.gov/government/fbci/2006_accomplishments.html

Wirt, Frederick M. 1971. "The politics of hyperpluralism." p. 101–125 in Howard S. Becker, ed., *Culture and Civility in San Francisco.* New Brunswick, N.J.: Transaction Books.

CHAPTER 4
The Skeleton of Power

1. What does it mean to say, "cities are creatures of the state?" Describe some of the ways this affects the locality in which you live.

2. Of the three forms of local government described in the chapter, which form is most like the one in which you live? Identify the person (or group) who has the power to appoint heads of departments. Who presides over meetings of the local legislative body?

3. Attend a meeting of your local government's council or commission. Describe the most important thing you learned from this experience. Was there any conflict going on during the meeting? Describe the issue involved in the conflict.

4. Identify a special district in or near the locality in which you live. What is the purpose of the special district? How was it created? Are its boundaries different from those of the local government? What are some of the advantages and disadvantages of this organization?

5. What steps are required to create a local government (incorporation) in your state? How difficult is it for a local government to annex additional territory into its jurisdiction? Describe the results of any recent incorporation and annexation by a municipality in your area.

CHAPTER 5
INFORMAL DECISION MAKING IN THE COMMUNITY

—*Harvey K. Newman*

Not all decisions are made at city hall. Imagine for a moment that two guys are on the putting green of the final hole of a golf course. One is holding the flag for another and says "Nice putt." The other replies, "Thanks, looks like I win today." The flag holder asks, "Where do you think we ought to build the new convention center? I think it ought to be near that parking deck I own." The other responds, "Yes, that sounds like a great place to enlarge our convention facility. We could attract more and larger groups. Maybe bring some new jobs to the area, and certainly help with the sales tax revenue. I'll discuss it with the mayor next week."

What is going on in the scene above? Local leaders were supposed to have a *formal* meeting at city hall or in the boardroom of an important corporation to make decisions. Instead, they are having an *informal* gathering on the golf course to decide how things will get done. Sometimes, when the formal meeting does take place, it is just to ratify the agreement made when a small group of the most influential people has talked among themselves in their private, less formal gatherings.

In most communities, people often meet in informal settings to make important decisions. These settings might include a private club, a gym, a bar, or wherever people gather and talk. How do these leaders have the power to make decisions during informal gatherings on a golf course? Is politics always about the backroom deals that shape decisions? This chapter describes how important decisions often get made in towns and cities most everywhere. The process of making local decisions through informal processes has been described as an "urban regime." In this chapter, the idea of a regime is used to provide an understanding of the way that these informal decisions are made.

A half century ago, the study of politics involved the analysis of formal structures of decision making. Students examined organization charts from city hall to see where the lines of authority connected one square on the chart to another. More recently, this study has taken a different turn recognizing how many decisions are made based on the tacit, informal agreements of people who interact with one another on a regular basis. The study of these kinds of informal coalitions is called regime politics. Political scientist, Clarence Stone, defined an urban regime as "the informal arrangements by which public bodies and private interests function together in order to be able to make and carry out governing decisions." (1989, 6) This notion of regime politics is helpful in figuring out who really makes decisions within a local community.

The first step in using regime theory to understand a town or city is to determine who the major participants are in local decision making. In the example of the two people on the golf course, these may be important business leaders. The cast of characters may vary from place to place and may change over time within the same place. In 1950, when Floyd Hunter studied decision making in Atlanta, he identified the forty most influential people in the city. Of these, twenty-nine were business leaders, so that leaders from government, community groups, and others represented only eleven of the forty. These forty leaders included only five females and one African American (Hunter, 1953). In recent years, the same kind of list would be very different. One constant would probably be that a majority of the leading decision makers would be from the private sector. Most local governments do not have the ability to accomplish their goals without the participation and cooperation of businesses. Since city governments by themselves lack the resources to govern and carry out important policies, local officials feel that they must keep existing businesses and try to attract new investment within their community in order to maintain local services and fiscal well-being.

On the other hand, businesses get involved in local politics for a variety of reasons. First, it may add to their profits to be part of a growing community—more investment usually translates into more jobs and people that can contribute to the prosperity of the city. Another reason for business involvement in local politics is to increase the value of their property. Involvement in local affairs can be valuable for the positive image of a business within a community, which can also increase profits. Business leaders often say they care about local government because it is the right thing to do.

There are often close personal ties between local elected public officials and business leaders. After all, many mayors and council members serve as part-time public officials, while retaining jobs in business organizations. Even full-time public officials often emerge from business backgrounds before their entry into the public sector, and many of these same individuals return to businesses after leaving office. These types of relationships insure that local governments most often pursue policies directed toward growth and investment in the local community. Political scientist, Paul Peterson, describes the type of policies favored most often by local governments as development policies (1981).

Local governments, most often with the support of business allies, pursue an agenda of development policies in order to attract or retain investment in the local area. It is generally assumed that the role of the public sector is to provide the setting for businesses to operate successfully within the boundaries of the government. For a city or town this means providing a good climate for business as well as incentives for business retention or attraction. After all, the local tax digest depends upon business investments in the community in order to provide revenues for public services as well as employment for local residents. Local public officials who are openly hostile or even indifferent to the needs of the private sector face the prospect of businesses relocating to other cities that might be more welcoming. This competition between towns and cities of all sizes for investment is another reason local governments must pursue development policies.

The two leaders on the golf course were discussing one type of economic development policy. Both favored building the larger convention center in order to attract more meetings to the city. Urban places both large and small are using variations of this policy to bring tourists with their dollars into their cities and towns. Places that are fortunate enough to have natural attractions are attempting to take advantage of these existing features such as the ocean, a riverfront, or lake shore to draw more leisure or recreation-oriented visitors. Other locations are seeking to become conference or convention locations and to attract more business travelers. A lack of natural attractions is not necessarily an obstacle for cities wishing to convert whatever assets they have into tourist amenities (Judd and Fainstein, 1999). These places must build the collection of facilities required for conferences or conventions.

The types of facilities that cities build to attract tourists are remarkably similar from place to place throughout the United States. One obvious need is for a hall large enough to host conventions or conferences. These facilities are almost always financed and built by the public sector as part of the infrastructure needed to attract visitors. Other common features of the tourist spaces in most cities include sports arenas for major or minor league games that can provide entertainment for locals as well as visitors. Festival malls such as Faneuil Hall in Boston, Harbor Place in Baltimore, and Underground Atlanta are also important components for a city's tourism business. These festival malls are developed to provide space to attract recreational shoppers rather than a resident population seeking mundane necessities. Most of these are the result of public subsidies by local governments in partnership with private investors. One of the earliest of these festival malls, Faneuil Hall in Boston required less than 21 percent public sector support, while Underground Atlanta received more than 80 percent of its funding from the public-sector. (Frieden and Sagalyn, 1989; Newman, 1999) Civic leaders hope that large public sector investments in meeting halls, sports arenas, and festival malls will encourage the spending of private dollars to build hotels, restaurants, and amusements for tourists.

In most towns and cities the efforts to attract visitors has replaced the earlier economic development policy of "smokestack chasing" by attempting to lure manufacturing plants to relocate from another town or region. For example, beginning soon after the Civil War, southern cities sought to entice the owners of textile mills to relocate their mills from the northeast. Many of these mills moved to the south taking advantage of cheaper labor and land costs as well as the subsidies offered by cities and states. More recently, many of these same plants have closed and relocated to other countries, leaving once thriving southern communities scrambling to attract new forms of investment through economic development policies focused on tourism.

Whereas the competition used to exist among towns to attract a textile mill or other type of industrial plant, many community leaders now seek tourists to visit, sleep, eat, drink, buy souvenirs, and perhaps find the locality pleasant enough to want to stay and do business. Local strategies vary from place to place. For instance, Marion, South Carolina was highly successful in attracting a diversity of industries that manufactured things ranging from candy to light bulbs. One by one, these plants began to close, leaving Marion County with the highest unemployment rate in the state from 2001 through the end of the decade. Local leaders were excited when two developers from Myrtle Beach decided to build a 27,000-seat amphitheater in Marion. The prospect of a $10 million investment and promises of 250 new jobs caused considerable enthusiasm among local elected public officials and business leaders (*Marion Star & Mullins Enterprise*, 28 March 2001, A-1&9). The town government was responsible for providing water and sewer lines for the facility as well as the same kind of investment incentives that might have been offered to an industrial plant. After this public and private investment, estimates of the crowd for the opening show in July 2001 ranged from 8,000 to 12,000, significantly less than half of total capacity, leaving many locals who put their money into vending permits and food to sell at the event unhappy with their investments (*Marion Star & Mullins Enterprise*, 11 July 2001, C-1; 18 July 2001, A-1 & 3). For most of its initial season in 2001, the amphitheater failed to attract the kinds of crowds that its promoters had hoped. Unfortunately, the following year, the amphitheater remained closed, dashing the hopes of local business and government leaders.

This cautionary tale from Marion, South Carolina could provide lessons for many other localities as they seek to become tourist destinations. Just as Flint, Michigan had a similar experience when its leaders sought to replace closed automobile manufacturing plants with a tourist theme park called AutoWorld, some towns and cities are just not attractive destinations for visitors. They not only lack natural attractions, these towns and cities also fail to provide the image of a place that visitors wish to experience. For these municipalities, it is a difficult task to construct the amenities needed for a tourist destination and expect visitors to come. Even with a theme park or a conference center plus nearby hotels, restaurants, and other amenities needed to attract visitors, some places are not regarded as favorable destinations by tourists. Local leaders in Flint, Michigan, for example, tried to build on the city's history with the construction of an automobile-themed amusement park and a new hotel in downtown, only to see both ventures fold quickly. The former director of Flint's AutoWorld described the failure of his city to attract tourists with these words, "You can't make Palm Beach out of the Bowery. If you want to make Palm Beach, you have to go to Palm Beach." (quoted in Judd, 2002, 296) Yet, to leaders of towns and cities everywhere, the possibilities of free-spending tourists coming to their communities provides a powerful stimulus to economic development policies of one kind or another designed to attract visitors. The result has been described as a "field of dreams" approach to economic development policy, with local business and political leaders believing "if we build it, the tourists will come." (Newman, 2002, 249)

Returning to our twosome of local leaders on the golf course, how are these local business people able to get things done? How are these particular leaders able to translate their conversation about the building of a new convention center into a decision that is both made and implemented? When Hunter studied decision making in Atlanta in 1950, he described a pattern in which a small group of business and professional people were able to dominate decisions in the city. Hunter called this pattern of decision making "elitism," and for his many followers, the pattern of communities controlled by a small elite group became the prevailing explanation of how cities are governed (1953). This small group of leaders would meet informally to decide on policies such as the use of transportation plans to expand the space of downtown. For example, one such private group of business leaders in Atlanta began planning the city's expressway system in 1948 (before the federal interstate highway system) with a curve in the north-south freeway that would serve two purposes. The land inside the bend would expand the space available for the expansion of downtown businesses, and the highway itself would form a barrier between downtown and the east Atlanta African-American residential area (Newman, 1999). Once the influential group of business leaders reached an informal agreement, they involved the mayor and other appropriate public officials to ratify and implement the agreement.

Other scholars disagreed with Hunter's claim that a small elite group of local business leaders was responsible for running a city. In his study of New Haven, Robert Dahl observed a variety of different individuals and groups participating in local decisions. One set of people would likely be involved in decisions involving transportation, while another set might make decisions in education, so that relatively different groups were involved in each policy area. Dahl called this pattern of governing "pluralism" after the diverse groups involved in each policy area (1961). The result was a vigorous debate between the elitists who followed Hunter and the pluralists who agreed with Dahl and saw more diversity among the participants in local decision making.

The debate ended in 1989 with the publication of *Regime Politics* by Clarence Stone. On one level, the study of decisions such as the construction of the new convention center by our golfing leaders might appear to be an elitist perspective. The two certainly represent large and powerful interests in the city. However, Stone is careful to distinguish between his position and that of Hunter's elitist point of view. For one thing, while these business leaders are often in a position to influence the outcome of decisions, they do not always get their way. Stone agrees to an extent with Dahl's pluralist point of view that decision making in a city is a process made complicated by a larger number of participants than the elitists might suggest. Thus, many less well-connected individuals could band together and influence decisions against the wishes of the business leaders.

Stone disagrees with the pluralists' view in his assessment of the importance of business groups within the regime. While Stone acknowledges that business groups do not always get their way, he understands that they are generally better organized and have more resources than other regime participants. These resources can include personnel, equipment, capital, and votes. Other groups who might take part in regime decisions include labor unions, nonprofit organizations, and religious groups such as churches, synagogues, and mosques, who can use their personnel and their ability to deliver votes to influence outcomes on particular issues. Few of these can match the resources of private sector businesses that have the people as well as the equipment and capital to influence local decisions with consistency over a long period of time. One question for thought and discussion is who are the organized groups that participate in decision making in your local community? Do all of these groups participate equally, or, is leadership on most issues provided by business organizations?

Stone has a different view from either the elitists or the pluralists on what business leaders *do* with their resources as decisions are made. There is a difference, for Stone, between the groups, like some of the ones listed above, who participate in certain regime decisions, and groups, like business interests, who are part of the regime itself because of their control of resources and the fact that they are "rarely absent totally from the scene." (1989, 7) Groups that participate in a regime do not use their resources to control decision making. Instead, the resources are used to produce cooperation among regime participants. This is an important distinction because both the pluralists and elitists examined the domination of local decision making and the costs of controlling the process. Regime politics is a study of how groups work together to achieve, in Stone's words, "cooperation of the kind that can bring together people based in different sectors of a community's institutional life and that enables a coalition of actors to make and support a set of governing decisions. . . . it is an examination of how that cooperation is maintained when confronted with an ongoing process of social change, a continuing influx of new actors, and potential break-downs through conflict or indifference." (1989, 8–9)

Stone refers to this process of groups working together to make and implement decisions as civic cooperation. His book is a case study of Atlanta in the post-World War II era, where an important social change was racial transition in the city as the population went from majority white to majority black between 1960 and 1970. Three years later, Atlanta residents elected their first African-American mayor, Maynard Jackson during a time in which the regime experienced a change from its older leadership to a new set of participants. Mayor Jackson experienced a variety of conflicts during his first two years in office (1974–1975). He imposed a vigorous affirmative action program in city hiring as well as joint venture and minority hiring requirements for businesses seeking contracts with the city. These actions brought a strong reaction from business leaders such as Harold Brockey of Rich's Department Stores, whose private letter to the mayor raising the possibility of white-owned businesses leaving downtown Atlanta was published by the *Constitution*. In his letter Brockey described the breakdown in civic cooperation saying, "the dilution of the partnership between government and business in Atlanta has resulted in a major communications-action vacuum." (*Constitution*, 21 September 1974, A-1) In other words, without the traditional partnership between city hall and business, things would not get done in Atlanta.

Group conflict between the mayor and business leaders continued with the newspaper publishing a series of seven articles with the headline, "Atlanta, a City in Crisis." These articles depicted the leadership of earlier white mayors as a golden age in the past when compared with the lack of cooperation between Mayor Jackson and the city's mostly white business leaders. One aspect of the conflict expressed in both the Brockey letter and the "City in Crisis" newspaper articles was the perception on the part of business leaders of a mayor who was letting downtown become overrun with criminals. Both sides quickly realized that the public conflict between the mayor and business leaders was bad for Atlanta's image. This realization led to vigorous efforts to promote an image of harmony between Mayor Jackson and business leaders. The mayor summarized these efforts to paint a picture of cooperation between the two sides in a speech to a Chicago audience where he said, "Atlanta can't prosper without city hall and business in bed together." (*Constitution*, 21 November 1974, A-1) The police chief added more patrols to the downtown area, and Mayor Jackson began a regular series of early morning breakfast meeting with business leaders that came to be known as the "Pound Cake Summits." (Newman, 2000) These actions promoted a greater level of cooperation between Mayor Jackson and downtown business leaders. Both sides recognized that they needed each other, and this realization paved the way for a better working relationship during Mayor Jackson's second term. The breakfast meetings provided the informal settings where discussions could take place that enabled the regime to function more effectively.

How do leaders such as the two golfers achieve the cooperation needed to get things done within the city? Stone's term "civic cooperation" describes the process of coordinating efforts across the boundaries of groups within a regime (1989, 184). Businesses, organizations, and individuals that support regime decisions are likely to benefit from their cooperation with the process. Those who are shut out or oppose the decisions being made usually suffer consequences for their actions. Incentives for participation might include access to employment, contracts, foundation support, and other benefits. Usually this system of incentives is based on an agreement among all the regime participants on the benefits of growth to the city. Sociologists, John Logan and Harvey Molotch, described this coalition as an urban growth machine in which all of the parties stand to benefit from local growth policies. Important growth machine participants would include business people who are involved in property investing, development, and real estate finance. This group includes lawyers, bankers, and others who benefit from increasing the value of land and buildings within a city. Less obvious growth machine participants would be local media such as newspapers, radio, and television stations that profit from growth through increased subscribers, listeners, and viewers as well as increased advertising revenue. Local public officials generally support the goals of bringing growth to the community as it tends to reflect favorably on their record in office and provides the benefits of increased tax revenues and employment. Utility companies that provide electricity, gas, water, and cable services stand to benefit from a growing community that brings new customers and increased demand for their services (Logan and Molotch, 1987).

In addition to the major players in the urban growth machine, Logan and Molotch identify a list of other supporters of local growth policies. These are labor unions, professional sports teams, and cultural institutions such as universities, museums, theaters, and symphonies in a locality. A growing community provides additional patrons for a symphony or a museum as well as additional financial supporters. Sports teams can increase their fan base within a growing city. Universities are increasingly regarded as engines of economic development for towns and cities. Prominent examples include the role of Stanford University in the development of the Silicon Valley in California and the three universities (Duke, University of North Carolina at Chapel Hill, and North Carolina State) which form the three points of the Research Triangle. Other growth machine participants may include corporate business leaders, self-employed professionals, and small retailers (Logan and Molotch, 1987).

An interesting question is the role that churches and other religious organizations play within local growth machines. Many small congregations form an important part of the neighborhoods in which they are located. Members who live in the area often participate in the activities of the congregation and develop close attachments to other members and to the institution itself as the place where births, weddings, funerals, and other events are observed over the course of years. Larger congregations may, however, sometimes find themselves at odd with the residents of the area in which their church is located. As congregations seek additional land for parking or buildings, neighbors may oppose these expansion plans as the church may bring unwanted traffic and congestion to the area. At other times, churches may act like full-fledged participants in the local growth machine in the pursuit of profits from the value of their land.

Usually, the members of a local growth machine are organized to promote local development through groups such as Chambers of Commerce, Convention and Visitors Bureaus, and other civic associations. Public officials who favor growth coalition interests receive campaign support and media endorsements. Nonprofit organization directors also depend on the financial support of individual business leaders as well as foundations that are responsible to many of these same business interests. This creates the system of selective incentives to promote civic cooperation which Stone describes with the phrase, "go along to get along." (1989, 192) Those who realize the benefits of going along with the coalition know that cooperation is rewarded and non-cooperation is punished. Punishment may take the form of withholding financial support or simply ignoring those who do not go along with the wishes of major regime participants. Either consequence can be harmful to groups such as small non-profit organizations that can be shut out of access to important sources of support and publicity for their programs. Individuals also take part in the same system of incentives to go along to get along.

The system of rewards and punishment that are part of civic cooperation do not just apply to individuals seeking personal opportunities within the growth coalition. It also extends to the broader question of how to further more complex projects and to promote policy initiatives. Advancing a project or program usually requires many forms of support ranging from money needed from several sources, endorsements, favorable publicity, and help from knowledgeable experts on how to avoid many technical and legal pitfalls. Business leaders are typically the source for this kind of assistance. The availability of their aid is usually indispensable for a local project or proposal to move forward. Likewise, opposition from these sources can kill a project (Stone, 1989). This system of civic cooperation gives business leaders an advantage when it comes to influencing local decisions. It does not mean that Hunter was correct in describing municipal decision making by a small elite.

Opposition to policies and programs favored by business interests frequently surfaces in towns and cities. Opponents face the difficulty of organizing themselves and producing enough resources to counter the efforts of a local regime. Remember that resources can take the form of people as well as money and other materiel. Thus, a large number of well-organized citizens can be effective in opposing the wishes of a smaller number of more well-to-do residents. Opposition can be expressed through votes in a local election. This can thrust forward a candidate who opposes the existing policies of a regime or its leadership. Once the election is over, the challenge becomes one of effective governance. This will require building longer term coalitions to make decisions rather than the relatively simple task of mounting opposition during an election.

One example of an election coalition may be seen in the 1973 campaign of Maynard Jackson for mayor of Atlanta. In his race against incumbent Sam Massell, Jackson put together a coalition of two sizable groups in the city. The first was the new majority of black citizens who responded to his progressive agenda of affirmative action and minority contracting. The second was a coalition of mostly young white voters who were part of an emerging neighborhood movement that opposed plans by the Georgia Department of Transportation and business leaders to build an expressway project known as I-485. The proposed roadway would run through several older neighborhoods as it connected downtown with Stone Mountain in the eastern suburb of DeKalb County. Jackson put together a successful electoral coalition of black voters and white neighborhood activists and defeated Mayor Massell. Once in office, however, the problem of implementing his policy agenda in the face of business opposition proved difficult. Some of the opposition during Jackson's first two years in office by the *Constitution* as well as other business groups and individuals has been described. Jackson's remaining six years as mayor were spent trying to repair relationships with business leaders. This was needed to provide the civic cooperation that would enable the traditional partnership between city hall and business leaders to continue to function in the city. Civic cooperation is a kind of glue that binds together participants in a regime.

The lesson of civic cooperation to build a governing coalition within the regime was not lost on Jackson's successor, Andrew Young. Young was familiar to voters after serving as congressional representative of the city and as ambassador to the United Nations under President Jimmy Carter. He ran for mayor with the support of Maynard Jackson and a solid majority among African-American residents. Most of the white downtown business leaders favored his opponent. The day after his election in 1981, Young addressed a luncheon of business leaders and told them, "I didn't get elected with your help, but I can't govern without you." (Stone 1989, 110) With this speech and his subsequent actions, Young won the support of the city's business leadership. Throughout his eight years as mayor, Andrew Young remained a strong partner with the city's business community in the traditional regime coalition. This occasionally put him into conflict with the interests of low-income, African-American residents of the city as well as white neighborhood activists. Young was able to pursue his agenda of economic development for the city with the active cooperation of business leaders. This resulted in the accomplishment of complex tasks such as the redevelopment of the downtown tourist attraction known as Underground Atlanta. Young used his skills and contacts as a former diplomat to encourage international investment in the city. He was also a major participant in the process of preparing the successful bid for Atlanta to host the 1996 Summer Olympic Games. If Logan and Molotch are correct, most mayors follow the pattern of Andrew Young of Atlanta in working closely with business leaders as part of the local growth coalition.

It seems obvious that our golfers are part of the local growth machine in their city. If so, what other lessons can be learned from our pair of leaders about regime decision making? One valuable lesson is *how* the participants in the regime get things done. Our golfers are important business leaders. To a degree these leaders control the agenda for the local community—whether the community is a smaller town or a city. Once the discussion starts on *where* to locate the new convention center, the debate already assumes that it is a good idea to build the facility. This ignores the larger issue of whether a new facility should be built at all. In this instance, control over the agenda helps to shape the outcome, so that little discussion is held on *if* a new convention facility should be built. Should, for example, the new facility be built on land owned by one golfer, or on the site of the older facility after it was demolished to make way for the new? No one seems to question whether convention visitors will want to come to town once the facility is built. It is often difficult for local leaders to recognize that sometimes the city they call home is not a place tourists want to visit no matter what kinds of attractions are constructed.

The private, informal discussion between our two leaders is, in itself, an important step in local decision making. It is increasingly recognized that the use of language by those in positions of power has the ability to shape actions. Beauregard suggested that the words of business and political leaders in a city have ethical consequences (1993). Those who are in a position to shape the discourse can use their position to define the actions of others within a locality (Foucault, 1982). This provides another powerful resource for those who are in a position to use it. Even though the discussions are held in informal settings, these conversations may later be favorably reported by local media who are generally supportive of growth policies and participants in regime decisions. Newspapers, for example, can play a neutral role in the discussion of which site to build the new convention center, but local media almost always favor policies that promote growth. In this way, the news media can also frame the discussion to avoid, or at least minimize, the issue of whether or not the city needs a new convention facility. Reporters can be sent out to investigate the pros and cons of each potential location—to build on the site of the parking lot owned by our golfer or to tear down the smaller old convention center and build the new facility on that site. Other issues such as job training for the under-employed or those without jobs and improving the quantity and quality of low- and moderate-income housing are more difficult to place on the agenda for public discussion within the community.

Does this mean that less well-connected citizens should become resigned to the fact that business leaders are usually going to get their way just because of their wealth and influence on informal decision making? Stone says that regime participants can change their minds about issues if they are made aware of opposing points of view. This is a process of changing the regime that Stone calls "social learning." (1989, 212) Perhaps one way to describe social learning is with the story of the mule and the 2-by-4 board. There was a time not so long ago when mules provided much of the power for agriculture in the United States. These creatures were known for their stubbornness. This meant that sometimes, when a mule refused to budge, the farmer had to hit the mule in the head with a 2-by-4 in order to get its attention. Changing the regime can be a bit like that. It is sometimes necessary to hit the mules in the head with a board in order to get their attention if you want them to go in a different direction. This is the process of social learning that may be required to get the attention of some rather stubborn mules. Social learning is the process of opening the eyes of regime participants to other points of view that might not have occurred to them otherwise.

Social learning can be done in a variety of ways without resorting to the use of 2-by-4s. One strategy is to provide regime leaders with information and education that they might not get from other sources. A simple strategy is to bring attention to an issue that needs the attention of local leaders. Individuals and groups can write letters, lobby elected officials, or even hold demonstrations to call attention to important issues. Another approach is through active participation on committees, boards, and commissions set up by local government.

One example of social learning took place during Andrew Young's two terms as mayor of Atlanta. From the moment of his election, Young formed a strong partnership with business leaders to promote development in the city. Some Atlanta residents who were left on the sidelines of regime decisions during the early years of Young's tenure as mayor were the advocates of historic preservation. Older commercial buildings and homes were usually torn down if they stood in the way of new development. Working quietly behind the scenes, the members of the city's Urban Design Commission sought to change the minds of those who believed that historic preservation always conflicts with development. Instead, the Commission members argued that the preservation of older structures could enhance their value. The lobbying of City Council members to support preservation efforts resulted in the passage of a three-month moratorium on demolition permits for historic buildings. This period was designed to give preservation advocates long enough to make their case for saving these older buildings.

Mayor Young argued that historic preservation would limit development in the city. He said that city policy should aim to "create a history of the golden age of integration and development, rather than preserving the old days of segregation and poverty." (Stone, 1989, 130) The mayor vetoed the proposed moratorium saying that preservation regulations might slow investment in the city by scaring off developers. Young also denounced one of the city's oldest apartment complexes as a "hunk of junk," that was not worth saving. This speech became a rallying cry for preservation advocates who responded with buttons and bumper stickers saying "Save the Hunk of Junk." Without the moratorium on demolition permits in place, the apartments and several other historic structures were torn down during 1986 (Newman, 2001).

Protests over the demolition of these older buildings continued to mount, and, in response, Mayor Young agreed to form a task force to develop a new preservation policy for the city. Along with four members of the city council, four developers, four preservation activists, and several other city officials, Young also served as a member of the task force. His presence assured that the meetings would be well attended, so these were scheduled when he was available. National experts on historic preservation and others appeared before the task force as the group met over the next two years. At the end of the process, the task force members developed a consensus in support of a new and stronger historic preservation ordinance for Atlanta. Both the preservationists and the developers compromised on some issues in order to arrive at the final policy proposal. What is more significant, during the process, the two sides developed lines of communication and a level of trust that would be needed to secure passage of the proposed ordinance by the city council. Finally, in June 1989, the city council passed the new historic preservation ordinance, and Mayor Young signed the legislation.

In Stone's terms, social learning took place over the course of the meetings by the task force members, so that both sides came to understand one another. Before the meetings of the task force, the participants on the two sides had viewed one another with suspicion, if not hostility. As a result of the process, the developers and Mayor Young were able to see the point of view of the preservationists that saving older buildings made economic sense and also contributed toward making the city a more interesting place (Newman, 2001). Stone described social learning as the capacity for members of the regime to inform themselves and to understand more diverse points of view so that decisions were not made exclusively within the confines of the selective incentives provided to regime participants.

The example of the task force on historic preservation shows how social learning can work. In this case social learning provided openness to more issues raised by the community with the potential to change the regime into a more inclusive coalition (Stone, 1989). After years of being able to ignore the wishes of preservationists, the process experienced by the task force resulted in the passage of the new ordinance and its approval by Mayor Young. As a result, older buildings continue to enjoy a higher level of protection as well as an improved procedure for dealing with threats to historic structures. Demolition of a building with historic significance is no longer done without a careful review of its merits and its potential for economic return for the owner. This was part of the compromise that resulted from the extensive meetings of the task force and the social learning by developers and elected public officials (Newman 2001).

Social learning can produce the benefits of an expanded range of vision by important decision makers. This can result in broader participation in the regime and, often, a change in regime policies. For a group of citizens to change the regime requires that they must know who the key participants are in the local regime. Armed with the names of important local business and political leaders, the citizens can proceed to the next step—organization. The old saying about there being strength in numbers applies to efforts to change local policies. First, there have to be large numbers of citizens wanting change, and, in addition, they must be well organized. This may mean strengthening existing organizations or perhaps forming new ones.

Organizational strength also comes from the willingness to form alliances with other partners in the city. Here the first rule is "you help me and I'll help you," as people representing varied interest groups join together in coalitions to secure benefits from local political action. Coalition politics can come from alliances between unlikely partners, but it is crucial to increase support by forming these types of informal alliances. This means that the second rule of political coalitions is "politics makes strange bedfellows." (Phillips, 1996, 388) These informal coalitions can be effective in seeking to influence decisions within a local regime.

One of the classic studies of coalition building in local politics was Chester Hartman's description of the contest over land use in the building of the proposed Yerba Buena convention center in San Francisco (1973). In his story, the plan for the new convention center was advanced by a powerful coalition of business leaders. The development advocates included tourist-oriented businesses, the local Hotel Owners Association, the Chamber of Commerce, and others who thought that the new convention center would be good for business in San Francisco. This coalition was well represented in the official local government agency known as the San Francisco Redevelopment Agency (SFRA), which was responsible for urban renewal and redevelopment in the city. The new center would be located in an area near downtown that consisted of low-income housing, warehouses, and older industrial plants that was known as Yerba Buena. The pro-development coalition funded studies designed to demonstrate how much San Francisco would benefit from the proposed center, they lobbied city officials to give the necessary approvals, and actively participated in planning the project. The prospect of jobs created by the construction of the new center attracted the support of labor unions, contractors, and others who joined the coalition supporting the convention facility. This familiar growth machine coalition came together around what each of the participants considered as their own self-interest in what they wanted, not only for themselves, but for what they regarded as good for the city as well.

Once the SFRA started the process of acquiring land, moving residents, and demolishing buildings in the Yerba Buena area, a reaction against the pro-growth coalition began. Neighborhood residents, who were mostly poor and elderly, established an organization known as Tenants and Owners in Opposition to Redevelopment (TOOR) to represent their interests. TOOR members demonstrated against the proposed convention center. They also filed a lawsuit to block the project, claiming that the center would destroy the neighborhood which had long been their home. TOOR argued that if the development did take place, area residents should receive new affordable housing near the old neighborhood, as well as social services, open space, and a voice in planning how their future neighborhood would be built.

The members of TOOR seemed like an uneven match for the well-organized pro-growth coalition. The group reached out to form their own coalition with partners that included environmentalists opposed to the development of the convention center and a taxpayer group who feared that the financing of the proposed convention center would increase local property taxes. Together these diverse opponents of the Yerba Buena Center were able to bring the project to a temporary halt. During this interval, the members of TOOR struck a compromise with the pro-growth coalition. TOOR ended its litigation against the city in return for its support of the proposed convention center. In return, TOOR received funding for affordable housing in the area as well as relocation benefits and improved social services. The convention center project was scaled down in size allowing more open space in the area which had been one of the concerns of the environmentalists. The smaller size of the project also reduced the cost of financing the center that had been the focus of the taxpayer group.

What are the lessons of the Yerba Buena case study for the understanding of coalition politics? First, successful coalition building can be part of the informal ways to use power in making local decisions. The rather strange coalition of opponents found enough strength in their numbers to change the outcome of the process in their favor. While the coalition did not succeed in stopping the project, it did have a positive influence on the outcome. Second, the results of the process showed the willingness of all of the participants to compromise. Neither side got all that it had initially wanted, but the results reflected the interests of many more of the city's residents than represented by the pro-growth coalition, or by the opposing groups alone. Next, the Yerba Buena case shows the influence of informal coalitions in local decision making. The city charter does not recognize the importance of business interests or organized citizens' groups in shaping policy. Yet, the informal coalitions were central to the process of shaping how the convention center would be built. The interests of the well-financed business organizations were important, but their strength and size did not guarantee that they would get their way. A well-organized, often diverse coalition opposed to a particular development project can influence the outcome in significant ways. In Stone's terms, this coalition can provide the social learning to change regime decisions. Finally, Hartman's case study is typical of the struggles that take place in towns and cities everywhere (Phillips, 1996). While the names of the projects and the participants may differ, coalition politics produce the drama that takes place in every locality.

One important reason to read newspapers and key web sites every day is to learn about what issues are important within the community. But, arming yourself with this information is merely an initial step. Local politics should not be a spectator sport that you watch from the sidelines. It calls for both individual and group participation. The more people who take an active part in local politics, the more representative and democratic your town or city's decision making is likely to be. Most citizens fail to realize just how important local politics is to their lives, and that we all have responsibilities as urban citizens.

Another sad fact is that few residents even know what their local government does for them. It could be argued that local politics does more to determine the quality of a resident's life than any other level of government.

This is not to minimize the importance of the national government and its role in defending our shores and representing the United States in relations with other countries. State governments also play a significant role in exercising powers not specifically delegated to the federal government. One of those important state powers is creating local governments. But, local governments are responsible for those issues that most directly affect the quality of our day-to-day lives. The list of services provided by local governments includes public safety (police and fire protection), parks, recreation, streets, sidewalks, water treatment, sewers, trash collection, and education. These are crucial things that touch our lives every day, which are generally ignored or given little attention as long as they are performed as a matter of routine. Only when the transit system breaks down, the sanitation workers go on strike, or we somehow experience an interruption in our services from local government that we notice how much each of us depend on these things that we normally take for granted.

As much as the routine services of local government affect our lives, we also need to take into account how our lives are touched by the kind of development policies, and other decisions, made by town, city, or county governments. The ways in which these decisions are made in each community, regardless of size, constitutes the local regime. The number of participants involved in making these policy decisions can vary from a minimum of two individuals, such as our golfers, upward to include as many citizens as possible.

Perhaps if citizens are informed about how the local regime in their city functions, the decision on the new convention center will not be made on the basis of *where* the facility ought to be located. Then, the discussion of the issue would not be limited to our pair of business leaders chatting on the golf course. (This might, in itself, be an argument in favor of more inclusive memberships in private golf clubs.) With more people brought into the discussions the question of *if* the community needs a new convention center will certainly be raised. Who would stand to benefit from the proposed new facility? Would the new facility affect low-income residents? Would it create new jobs, and, if so, how many and what kind of employment would the convention center generate? Would the facility bring in revenue from tourist dollars? What evidence is there to indicate that large numbers of tourists will want to come to our city? What would a new facility cost? How would it be financed? Would voters have a chance to approve both the construction and the financing of the convention center? In many towns and cities, decisions such as these are made behind closed doors within development authorities that are shielded from public review. Would taxpayers be responsible for paying any shortfall if rental income from the use of the facility turns out to be less than anticipated? These are the kind of questions that a fuller and more open discussion of the convention center proposal ought to include.

As many people as possible need to be personally involved in these kinds of discussions, and citizens have a responsibility to bring others to the table to participate as well. Broader regime participation could provide the kind of social learning that Stone suggested. This would bring changes in the regime itself and in the kinds of discussions that are carried on when decisions are made. Stone's book, *Regime Politics* is dominated by an image of society that lacks consensus. People are not bound together by an integrating body of thought, a shared idea of the world, or even a set of norms and values that most share. Instead, society is loosely bound together at best, and usually fragmented into an arena such as a city where interest groups must be brought together in order to produce any sort of policy result. The process of making decisions is the task of bringing together enough resources to influence, first, policy making and, then, policy implementation. Governance takes place by the act of bringing groups together in order to act (Stone, 1989).

Understanding the regime in the town or city provides a way to navigate the process of decision making wherever you live. It should serve as a reminder to us all that we are urban citizens who have the obligation not only to participate in local decisions ourselves, but to bring others to participate. All kinds of local organizations can serve as bridges between people within the community to provide social learning, so that decisions are not made in the shadows and the backrooms, but with the greater social learning among groups that is a result of broader participation in local government.

REFERENCES

Beauregard, Robert A. 1993. *Voices of decline: The postwar fate of US cities.* Cambridge, UK: Blackwell.

Dahl, Robert A. 1961. *Who governs?* New Haven, CT: Yale University Press.

Foucault, Michel. 1982. The subject and power. In *Michel Foucault: Beyond structuralism and hermeneutics,* eds. H. L. Dreyfus and P. Rabinow, 208–226. Chicago: University of Chicago Press.

Frieden, Bernard J. and Lynne B. Sagalyn. 1989. *Downtown Inc.: How America rebuilds cities.* Cambridge, MA: MIT Press.

Hartman, Chester. 1973. *Yerba Buena: Land grab and community resistance in San Francisco.* San Francisco: Glide Press.

Hunter, Floyd. 1953. *Community power structure: A study of decision makers.* Chapel Hill: University of North Carolina Press.

Judd, Dennis R. 2002. Promoting tourism in US cities. In *Readings in urban theory,* 2nd ed., eds. Susan S. Fainstein and Scott Campbell, 278–299. Malden, MA: Blackwell.

Judd, Dennis R., and Susan S. Fainstein, eds. 1999. *The tourist city.* New Haven, CT: Yale University Press.

Logan, John R. and Harvey L. 1987. *Urban fortunes: The political economy of place.* Berkeley: University of California Press.

Newman, Harvey K. 1991. God and the growth machine. *Review of Religious Research* 32, no. 3 (March): 237–243.

_____. 1999. *Southern hospitality: Tourism and the growth of Atlanta.* Tuscaloosa and London: University of Alabama Press.

_____. 2000. Hospitality and violence: Contradictions in a southern city. *Urban Affairs Review* 35, no. 4 (March): 541–558.

_____. 2001. Historic preservation policy and regime politics in Atlanta. *Journal of Urban Affairs* 23 (1): 71–86.

_____. 2002. Decentralization of Atlanta's convention business. *Urban Affairs Review* 38, no. 2 (November): 232–252.

Peterson, Paul E. 1981. *City limits.* Chicago: University of Chicago Press.

Phillips, Barbara E. 1996. *City lights: Urban-suburban life in the global society.* New York: Oxford University Press.

Stone, Clarence N. 1989. *Regime politics: Governing Atlanta, 1946–1988.* Lawrence: University Press of Kansas.

Chapter 5
Informal Decision Making in the Community

1. Select an example of an important decision that has been made in your community. Who were some of the major participants in the process of making the decision? Describe any groups or prominent individuals who either supported or were opposed to the decision.

2. Describe an effort in your community to promote economic development by attracting tourists. Who were some of the important participants in this decision? Assess what evidence you can find to indicate if the project is a success.

3. The Yerba Buena case study from San Francisco has a number of important lessons for all communities. Select a development proposal that has been made in your community. Who are some of the informal coalition members who have emerged to support the issue and to oppose the proposal? Are their compromises that were made by coalition participants during the process? How did the informal coalitions influence the final outcome?

4. Social learning is a term used by Stone to describe how a regime can be changed. Describe an example of how social learning changed how a decision in your community was made. What single person or group provided the social learning in your example?

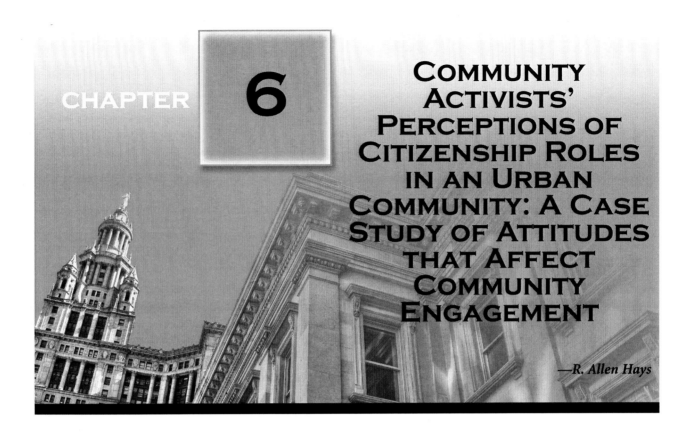

CHAPTER 6

COMMUNITY ACTIVISTS' PERCEPTIONS OF CITIZENSHIP ROLES IN AN URBAN COMMUNITY: A CASE STUDY OF ATTITUDES THAT AFFECT COMMUNITY ENGAGEMENT

—R. Allen Hays

ABSTRACT

This chapter addresses the linkages and barriers between civic participation and political participation in urban communities, through a qualitative case study of the attitudes of community activists in a small urban community. Robert Putnam's theoretical model of civic and political involvement suggests a strong linkage between civic engagement and political engagement, while Nina Eliasoph's model suggests substantial barriers between participation in the local civic realm and participation in the local political realm. These competing models are given a preliminary test utilizing in depth interviews with a cross section of persons who are actively involved in the civic and/or the political realms. The data confirm Putnam's assertion of the strong linkage between the two, but they suggest that the two arenas are viewed as distinct by activists and that the rewards derived from civic engagement are quite different from those of political engagement. The analysis also suggests that community activists have strongly negative views of those who do not participate and that their suggestions for involving others have limited utility. This barrier may be the strongest of all in preventing both civic and political engagement in the urban community.

> "MY FAITH TELLS ME THAT MY ABILITIES ARE GIFTS AND THAT I HAVE A RESPONSIBILITY TO USE THEM FOR COMMUNITY BETTERMENT. I MUST SHARE MY BLESSINGS WITH OTHERS. FAITH WITHOUT ACTION IS DEAD. IT IS THROUGH ACTIONS, NOT WORDS, THAT FAITH IS TRULY EXPRESSED."
>
> NEIGHBORHOOD ACTIVIST

Direct Correspondence to: R. Allen Hays, Director of the Graduate Program of Public Policy, University of Northern Iowa, Cedar Falls, 1A 50614-0173. E-mail: allen.hays @ uni.edu.

"WHEN I SEE A NEED, I HOPE TO HELP. I AM VERY LUCKY TO HAVE THE PRIVILEGES I DO. I HAVE A RESPONSIBILITY TO GIVE BACK. IF I AM NOT WILLING, WHO WILL BE? ONE PERSON *CAN* MAKE A DIFFERENCE."

YOUNG HOMEMAKER, COMMUNITY SERVICE VOLUNTEER

INTRODUCTION

This chapter presents a case study of the attitudes of persons active in civic and political affairs in a small metropolitan community. It explores how these locally active citizens view the relationship between civic engagement (defined here as participation in voluntary, community-based organizations and associations) and political participation (defined here as individual and organizational attempts to influence public policy or the electoral process.) Do they perceive a distinct boundary between political and non-political community action, and does that boundary act as an obstacle to full political engagement? In addition, this paper will explore their perceptions of the obstacles that prevent civic and political action among a large segment of the population. Through a more complete understanding of how those who are already engaged understand the political process, one may better understand how those obstacles might be overcome.

These are important questions for urban scholars, because it is in the local, place-based political arena that citizens can often have their most direct impact on policy outcomes. While the issues addressed locally may ultimately be global in nature, they frequently appear most real to the individual citizen through their impact on the local community. Therefore, the local arena is more likely to be a comprehensible and satisfying arena for citizens than the larger national and international realm, and it becomes a training ground for the development of skills and attitudes necessary for ongoing participation. In light of the increasing public and scholarly concern over declining civic and political engagement, the study of participation in urban communities becomes critical not only to an understanding of how these communities function, but to an understanding of how civic participation functions in general.

CIVIC ENGAGEMENT AND POLITICAL PARTICIPATION

The recent increase in research on social capital and civic engagement has benefited urban scholarship by refocusing attention on a problem with which urbanists have long been concerned; namely, how citizens can be engaged and mobilized to exert effective influence on community decisions. With the exception of a few who have argued that too much participation may have a negative impact on urban policy making (Yates, 1980), most urban scholars believe that increasing citizen involvement is desirable, in that it is likely to lead to a more equitable distribution of the benefits of urban life among citizens. Even though economic elites inevitably play a powerful role in community decisions, citizen participation can provide a counterbalance to their influence. A number of urban scholars have described cities in which effectively and permanently organized citizens' groups have become part of the local regime that shapes each city's response to the demands of the international political economy (Berry, Portney, & Thompson, 1993; Stone, 1989).

The civic engagement literature has also broadened our concern from strictly political participation (defined here as participation intended to directly influence public policy or electoral outcomes) to include other forms of civic engagement (defined as participation in voluntary, community-based organizations and associations.) Robert Putnam, in his study of the differential functioning of similar local government institutions in different parts of Italy (1993), concluded that the presence of a civil society that embodied norms of trust, reciprocity, and obligation to the public good was vital to the success of these institutions. In turning his "social capital" analysis towards his own country, Putnam (1995, 2000) joined a growing group of scholars who have called attention to the decline of civic engagement in American communities and the negative implications of this decline for the political process (Barber, 1998; Etzioni, 1998; Skocpol & Fiorina, 1999; Woolcock & Narayan, 2000).

These scholars have identified "civil society" as a realm of informal ties and relationships distinct from both the market and the state. In their view, the absence of the profit imperative of the market and of the coercive elements of the state in this civic realm frequently enables decision making that is both flexible and public spirited (Bellah, 1985; Etzioni, 1998). Woolcock (1998) describes civil society as "the forums in and through which there is an attempt to harmonize, where necessary, the conflicting demands of individual interests and social good" (p. 190). Because of its informality and flexibility, civil society is a prime arena for the development of social capital. However, while defining civil society as distinct, these scholars have also argued strongly that citizens' engagement in the civic realm is *strongly linked* to their active and constructive political involvement. They assert that, if civil society is unhealthy, then the functioning of the political process will be impaired (Hooghe & Stolle, 2003). The citizen's engagement in political activity is grounded in his or her experiences within the social and civic realm. According to Putnam (2000), the influence of other variables affecting participation, such as socioeconomic status, is mediated by effective social capital formation in the civic realm.

Civic engagement has been linked to political engagement in at least four ways: (1) Civic engagement draws the citizen out of strictly personal concerns and into a greater awareness of shared, community needs; (2) civic engagement develops skills in organizing and mobilizing people that are transferable to the political realm; (3) civic engagement develops individual feelings of confidence and efficacy that make political activism more likely. (4) civic engagement develops networks of relationships (the interpersonal aspect of social capital) and feelings of trust (the attitudinal aspect of social capital) that are critical to effective political action. (See Lin, 2001 on the link between formal institutions and social networks.)

However, work by other scholars calls into question the degree to which civic engagement and political engagement are directly linked. Edwards and Foley (1997) argue that whether or not social capital translates into personal or political efficacy for an individual is *context specific*. That is, relationships that constitute effective social capital in one arena may not translate into efficacy in other arenas. In addition, the structure of the political economy (including such factors as the distribution of wealth and access to decision-makers) and the nature of the political culture, in which civil society is imbedded, may affect how well the relationships developed in this "independent" sector translate into effective political action (Skocpol, 1996, 2000).

A far stronger critique of the linkage assumption, a critique that focuses on the attitudinal dimensions of the relationship between group membership and political action, comes from Nina Eliasoph (1998). Eliasoph became a participant/observer in three groups: a country/western dance club that was strictly social in its purposes; a parent/teacher organization that embodied traditional "volunteerism"; and a locally based environmental organization that had explicitly political goals. She found that the norms of the social group actively *discouraged* serious discussion of political issues and promoted an attitude of cynical disengagement from the political process. Within the volunteer parent/teacher group, participants were discouraged from exploring the political dimensions of their work. The group focused on voluntary fund raising for "extras" at the school and squelched one individual's attempt to get them involved in the more political issue of public school funding. Moreover, even the overtly political environmental group tended to publicly frame issues in terms of narrow, personal concerns, rather than broader policy concerns; for example, by referring to themselves as "parents concerned about the effects of pollution on their children" rather than citizens concerned with the larger issue of environmental degradation. She refers to these tendencies to suppress political concerns as "political evaporation" (Eliasoph, 1998, pp. 6–9).

Eliasoph demonstrates that the anti-political nature of these groups *does not* stem from individual members' lack of awareness or concern with broader issues. In one-on-one interviews, group members often displayed a deep concern with, and a reasonably sophisticated analysis of, the impact of public policy decisions on their lives. Rather, it was *group norms* that kept these concerns and insights "backstage" and dictated that the "frontstage" activities of the groups would be non-political, anti-political, or limited in political scope. Members believed they had to follow these norms in order to be accepted by the group and to be effective in the public realm. Even though she addresses norms within the specific groups that she observed, it is reasonable to assume that individuals will carry these norms into other groups with which they become involved, so that the norms about political discourse that she observes may be treated as generalized attitudes towards participation held by individuals who are active in the community.

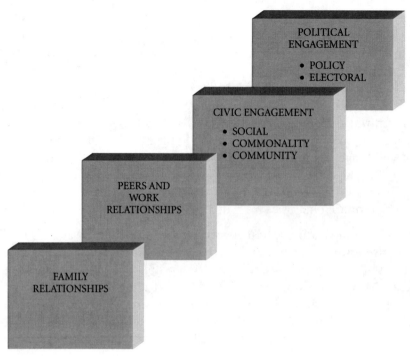

FIG. 6.1 | *Zones of Engagement.*

Eliasoph's analysis thus directly challenges the assumption that non-political engagement and social capital formation translates easily or automatically into a foundation for political engagement. In her view, participation in these groups is actually *toxic* to engagement in the broader political realm or to engagement in issues that are not in a citizen's backyard. Applying her perspective to urban community politics, one might expect that people who are engaged in socially beneficial activities that are traditionally associated with "volunteerism" might internalize norms that discourage them from extending their community involvement into the political realm. While the scope of her in-depth, qualitative study is necessarily limited, her work challenges us to view the linkage between civic participation and political participation as an empirical question to be examined, rather than an unexamined assumption underlying inquiry.

Obviously, neither Putnam's nor Eliasoph's perspective is likely to be entirely correct. What is needed is an analytical framework that facilitates the study of these linkage issues in community politics. As a first step towards such a framework, I propose the notion of "zones of engagement." These zones are shown schematically in Figure 1. Each zone has an invisible boundary that individuals must cross psychologically and behaviorally by shifting their commitment of time and energy to different activities and relationships. The first two zones are included in the model (and will be briefly described) in order to make it comprehensive, but they are not the focus of investigation in this chapter. Instead, this analysis focuses on the relationships between the civic and political zones of engagement. By examining the strength of the attitudinal barriers between these two zones, one may shed light on the willingness of individuals to transfer their time and energy from the civic into the political realm, and one may assess how valuable the full development of the civic realm really is to broadening political participation.

The most intimate zone of engagement is the family, through which humans are first nurtured and first become conscious of their interdependence with others. Most people devote a large amount of time and energy to family relationships, whether in their families of origin or in the nuclear families that they form as adults. Putnam argues that there has been a destructive decline in social capital within the family, which he attributes to our TV-obsessed, consumer culture. (Putnam, 2000, 216–246) The literature on political socialization also emphasizes the importance of familial attitudes in shaping later political participation (Erikson & Tedin, 2003, pp. 119–123). In addition, Stolle (2000) cites research from several countries indicating the importance of the values communicated by the family in building the social trust that is the basis for social capital formation.

Most individuals move outward from family relationships into informal relationships with peers, and into the formal relationships of education and employment. These relationships also make a large claim on their available waking hours, leaving other forms of engagement to their limited discretionary time. Putnam suggests that families with two adult wage earners in demanding jobs and families whose home, work, and leisure are widely separated geographically, have the most difficulty setting aside time for civic involvement (Putnam, 2000, pp. 204–216). In contrast, the political socialization literature suggests that occupational ties provide numerous opportunities for engagement in public policy issues and that peer groups often help citizens to process political information (Erikson & Tedin, 2003). However, a boundary clearly exists between the concerns of job and peers and engagement in the broader social and political arena.

The next zone of engagement is civic participation. By this is meant participation in non-governmental, voluntary associations that address common problems or needs. National surveys show that a majority of Americans belong to at least one volunteer association outside of family and work, despite recent declines in such memberships (Putnam, 2000).

Voluntary associations may be observed to fall into three broad categories. One category consists of social groups devoted to sports or a hobby. These are extended peer groups, in which the pursuit of some common interest—say stamp collecting or genealogy—facilitates satisfying social ties. They are directed at no societal purpose other than the intrinsic satisfaction of the activity. A second category consists of commonality groups, in which citizens band together to address an immediate, common problem. For example, people suffering from the same disease or disorder may form a support group, in order to exchange information and emotional support. Or, people may band together to clean up and beautify their neighborhood. A third category consists of community service groups. These are directed at some larger community good, one which does not directly benefit its members but which provides the satisfaction of making their community better (in whatever way they may define "better"). These groups may focus on quality of life improvements, such as promoting the arts, or they may focus on helping other citizens who are disadvantaged by poverty or disability.

The second and third types of voluntary groups are both potential bridges into the political realm. Group members may come to view action or inaction by government as an obstacle to achieving their goals. In the case of the disease group, they may protest lack of public funding for research or lack of access to treatment of their disease. (For example, see Casamayou, 2002 on the development of women's activism against breast cancer.) The neighborhood group may protest weak code enforcement by the local government as an obstacle to their clean up efforts. For groups supporting the arts, or trying to ameliorate poverty, the role of public policy in promoting solutions can easily become apparent. Moreover, as noted earlier, the skills and attitudes formed within these groups may be conducive to political action, not just on group concerns but on other concerns that may come to the individual's attention. However, the citizen must cross the invisible boundary between private, voluntary efforts, and efforts directed at public policy, and Eliasoph's research points to the attitudinal barriers that make crossing that boundary difficult.

Groups or individuals who enter the political zone can be either issue oriented or electorally oriented, and they can address issues at the local, state, national, or international level. Once they move past the local and state level, members often lose the benefit of face-to-face contact with other members, and their participation may be limited to writing checks to support professional staffers who pursue the group's goals. Putnam dismisses this "check book" participation as not generating meaningful engagement. On this point, he has been strongly challenged by interest group scholar Jeffrey Berry, who argues that national memberships are an important declaration of political identity and the only realistic way for individuals to exert influence on national policy decisions (Berry, 1999). Nevertheless, the immediacy of interpersonal contacts at the local level certainly gives them a transformative power that is less likely to be present in the more indirect and impersonal contacts of the national or international realm.

Whatever their mode of political participation, citizens have clearly entered a different realm than that of private, voluntary associations. Even at the local level, the political realm requires a broader; more abstract view both of the origins of problems and of their solutions, because fundamental distributional issues are raised. Consequently, it may require the time-consuming acquisition of complex substantive or procedural knowledge in order to master the issues. Direct, personal experience is no longer as clear a guide to action. In addition, political activity may expose the citizen to intense conflict and controversy, with which many are extremely uncomfortable, and, in some cases, it may expose them to criticism and sanctions by peers or in the workplace for getting involved in "controversial" issues. The fact that much lower percentages of citizens are politically active than are involved in voluntary associations suggests that the boundary between civic and political engagement is one that many citizens are loathe to cross (Verba, Schlozman, & Brady, 1995). While the other boundaries delineated in Figure 1 are very important, it is this civic/political boundary that is the primary focus of the research reported in this paper.

RESEARCH DESIGN
Propositions

The present research consists of an exploratory case study, utilizing embedded data consisting of the activities and attitudes of a group of community activists in Waterloo/Cedar Falls, Iowa, a metropolitan area of 125,000 (Yin, 1994). Based on the literature review just provided, five propositions have been developed for preliminary exploration utilizing what Yin (1994) refers to as the "pattern-matching" research design. The propositions are stated in such a way that empirical support for the propositions will reinforce the case for Eliasoph's view that the political and the civic realms are separated by clear boundaries, while a lack of support for the propositions will strengthen the case for Putnam's view that the two are closely interrelated. The purpose of this research is to gain a qualitative understanding of the degree to which those involved in a local community frame and understand their political and civic involvement in the terms suggested by these propositions. Full testing and confirmation of these propositions will, of course, require further research based on larger, random samples.

Proposition 1: A behavioral boundary exists between civic and political involvement. The patterns of involvement of community activists will reflect a clear boundary between civic activities and political activities to the extent that a different group of community activists is involved in each realm. If persons identified as active in the private, voluntary realm are also active in the local political realm (and vice versa) this will indicate a boundary that is less rigid.

Proposition 2: An attitudinal boundary exists between civic and political engagement. A clear boundary between civic and political activities will be reflected in the extent to which activists experience different rewards and frustrations from participating in each realm. Because the political realm tends to be more conflictual, it is anticipated that rewards will be derived from the victory of one's policy position or candidate over opposition, whereas in the civic realm, rewards will be derived from mutual problem solving. Also, a clear boundary will be reflected in the extent to which participants in each realm view participation in the other realm in a negative light.

Proposition 3: A motivational boundary exists between civic and political participation. A clear boundary between the civic and political realm will be reflected in somewhat different motivations for activity in each realm. The personal motivations that drive people to become involved and that keep them involved through the inevitable frustrations and failures that accompany activism will be different in each realm.

Proposition 4: The skills and attitudes acquired through civic participation will be somewhat different than those acquired through political participation. To the extent that the learning process in the civic realm reinforces negative attitudes towards political participation, civic participation will not lead to political participation. To the extent that common skills and attitudes are acquired through both activities, participation in one arena will encourage participation in the other.

Proposition 5: An attitudinal boundary exists between active political and civic participants and those who do not participate in community affairs. The attitudes of the respondents will reflect a clear distinction between their active participation and the non-participation of the majority of citizens. They will attribute different values to those who are inactive than to themselves and they will view the attitudes of non-participants negatively. They will also have definite ideas about how non-participants can be induced to participate more actively.

The Community

Historically, the Waterloo/Cedar Falls, Iowa metropolitan area grew on the basis of blue-collar industries, such as farm equipment manufacture and meat packing. Those industries remain important but, as with manufacturing in other parts of the United States, they are a declining percentage of the workforce, while service industries have increased. In the 1990s, the area recovered much of its economic health after a deep economic crisis in the 1980s (triggered by the farm crisis) but its population is currently stable, rather than growing. Due to the immigration of African Americans from the South in the 1920s, and due to a more recent influx of Latino workers attracted by the meat packing industry, Waterloo is the most ethnically diverse city in Iowa. According to the 2000 U.S. Census, approximately 14% of the population is African American and 2% is Latino.

Methods

In-depth, in-person interviews utilizing open-ended questions were conducted with 40 individuals who are active in various aspects of community life in the metro area. The interviewers made an effort to elicit the most detailed and complete answers possible from each subject. Interviews ranged in length from 45 to 90 minutes, depending on the extent to which the subjects chose to elaborate. While the interviews were structured to explore the propositions listed above, the questions allowed the subject maximum freedom to articulate her or his own understanding of the civic and political realms. Also, the interviews were designed to provide multiple opportunities for subjects to reflect on their involvement from different angles. In the case of civic participation, subjects were asked both about their most important organizational involvements and about their involvement in specific projects for the organizations in which they are active. In the case of political participation, subjects were asked about both issue oriented and electorally oriented political involvement.

In order to test the underlying causes of civic participation, a comparison group of inactive citizens would be necessary. However, that is not the purpose of this study. *Rather, its purpose is to explore how those who are already active frame their civic and political environment and whether their way of framing it corresponds to what might be expected based on the literature.* The extensive activism of most of these respondents has given them plenty of opportunities to reflect on their experiences. The barriers and difficulties that they have experienced have not prevented them from being involved, yet those same barriers might prove insurmountable to others. By understanding these barriers, one may gain insight into how those not involved might be guided towards involvement. In addition, those who are currently active may or may not be effective in providing openings and encouragement for others to become involved. By understanding their attitudes towards the majority of their fellow citizens who are much less active, one may gain a better understanding of how activists may play a more effective role in broadening participation.

Sample

During the last 20 years, this researcher has been extensively involved in community affairs in Waterloo/Cedar Falls; with local government and non-profits as a consultant, and with neighborhoods as director of my university's Community Outreach Partnership Center. These contacts have led to considerable knowledge about who is active in the community. This cross-sectional sample was selected based on this knowledge, plus consultation with key informants in areas of community life where I have been less involved. *In this study, a community activist is defined as a person who has displayed active involvement or leadership in at least one private, voluntary organization or in at least one political organization during the last five years.* Most respondents have been active in numerous organizations. Because of the small size of the metro area, a reasonable assessment of community activists with a sample of this size is possible.

Interview subjects were selected with the aim of providing a demographically representative cross section of community activists. Of those interviewed, 16 (40.0%) are white females; 13 (32.5%) are white males; four (10.0%) are African-American females; four (10.0%) are African-American males; two (5.0%) are Latino females; and one (2.5%) is a Latino male. These proportions are reflective of the overall community, except that white males were under-sampled. More Latino interview subjects would also have been desirable, even though Latinos are recent arrivals to the community, and, hence, are not yet as active as other groups in community affairs.

In terms of employment, 23 (57.5%) of the respondents are currently employed full time, while 12 (30.0%) are retired. Four interviewees (10.0%) are employed part time, and another is a full time homemaker. Thirty-five (87.5%) of the respondents have either a Bachelor's or a graduate degree, while the rest have either some college or a high school diploma only. With regard to age; 17.5% are under 40; 55.0% are between 40 and 60; and 27.5% are over 60. With regard to political orientation, 52.5% were classified as "liberal," 25.0% were classified as "moderate," and 22.5% were classified as "conservative". The fact that this group is older and better educated than the average citizen reflects, in large part, the general nature of political activists in American society and in this community.

The sample contains individuals whose activities span a full range of community endeavors. Some have been active in neighborhood associations, others in civic groups, others in arts groups, others in organizations addressing poverty, and still others have been primarily active in the political arena. A few are wealthy business leaders who have connections and influence within community-wide groups, while other respondents are working class folk whose primary arena of action has been their neighborhoods.

RESULTS
Community Service

Respondents were asked to list up to four voluntary community service activities in which they had engaged in the past 3 years. Many of these individuals are also employed in community service agencies, but the focus of this question was on *volunteer* involvement. The initial question about involvement was open-ended, allowing respondents to define what they considered to be "community service." Therefore, they could spontaneously mention any of the types of community activities specified in the discussion of Figure 1, including purely social groups and political activities as forms of community service. The sample included some individuals who are primarily identified as political activists and some that are mainly known for their civic involvement, so that the level of crossover between civic and political activities could be determined. As a result, one could expect that a significant number of political activities would be mentioned in these initial responses. One could also expect that some civic activities would be directed towards broad community purposes while some would be social or recreational in nature.

Reported activities were classified into three categories: political, civic, and social. (The two subcategories of "civic" mentioned above were combined in this analysis since one cannot consistently distinguish activities that are personally beneficial from those that solely benefit others without considerably more knowledge of the respondents than was acquired in the interviews. In some cases, respondents volunteered that they were personally affected by an issue.) A total of 24 (60.0%) of the respondents included no political activities among the four voluntary service activities they were asked to list. Of these, 18 (45.0% of the total) listed only civic activities, while the rest (15.0%) listed various combinations of civic and social activities. Of those who reported political activities (which included everything from organizing around issues to actual service as an elected official), nine (22.5% of the total) listed only one political activity, six (15.0%) listed two political activities, while only one (2.5%) listed three political activities.

This breakdown suggests that most respondents, whether known as political leaders or not, chose to report all or most of their activities in the civic realm when asked about voluntary service, with relatively few political activities mentioned, and even fewer in the social realm. They clearly identify the civic realm with voluntary service. However, these data do not reveal a distinct group of solely political activists who do not engage in civic volunteerism. Those who put a lot of energy into politics also report other forms of voluntary service. For example, one respondent, an African-American male, listed his service as an elected official as one of his civic activities, but his other activities included service on the non-profit boards of a local hospital and a local private college. Another respondent, a white senior male, reported his extensive activity in the Democratic Party, but he also mentioned his position on the board of a local nature preserve, and his role as an advocate for the mentally handicapped. For these and other activists, the boundaries between civic and political engagement appear rather porous, and Proposition 1 is not supported.

Collectively, these 40 individuals listed 149 voluntary activities in their responses to the first open-ended question about their involvement. (Percentages given below refer to *activities*, not individual respondents.) Although a few listed less than four, most could have easily listed more. Of the activities listed as community involvement, 19 (12.8%) could be classified as "political or governing," making this the largest single category of responses. The fact that many respondents volunteered political activities under the category of civic engagement also suggests that Proposition 1 is not valid for these respondents.

Nevertheless, the vast majority of activities listed by respondents fall into the category of civic involvement, rather than political involvement. Volunteer activities directed at general community improvement, rather than at a specific group such as the poor, are the most frequently cited (11.4% of the total). Examples include the Exchange Club; the Rotary; the United Way; the YWCA; and volunteer involvement in the city's Department of Leisure Services. Organizations devoted to the arts and culture were the next most frequently cited (10.1% of all activities.) Examples include the library board; various historical activities (including, in one case, Civil War reenactment); and organizing roles in arts and music festivals. (A typical case is a white female respondent who plays a key role in organizing a local jazz festival every year.)

In addition to these general community service organizations, involvement in groups serving the poor is frequently mentioned, constituting 10.1% of all activities. Examples include Habitat for Humanity and a community-wide poverty elimination effort known as Opportunity Works, Inc. Various human rights and social justice organizations also receive several mentions, such as, for example, Amnesty International and the National Association for the Advancement of Colored People (NAACP). Finally, involvement in neighborhood associations is mentioned by a number of respondents. For example, one black female respondent served as president of a coalition of neighborhood associations, while another served as secretary/treasurer for her neighborhood association.

Only a small number of purely social activities are classified by respondents as community service, and some of those have civic implications. For example, one African-American woman is active in a cotillion club for African-American girls. While this might seem a purely social activity, she emphasizes that the goals of the club are community oriented, in that its activities are designed to foster self-esteem among the girls and to help them develop social skills, so that they will be more successful later in life. She says of the club, "It gives [African-American] girls recognition that they don't often get. It is a highlight for them." Other activists may also belong to hobby groups, but they don't spontaneously classify them as "civic." For these respondents, the civic realm is clearly a realm of public service.

These respondents' commitment to their activities tends to be long term, with a mean period of involvement of 8.2 years. In addition, many of the activities cited were ones in which they had risen to leadership positions. Over half of the respondents (55.7%) were currently serving or had served as a board member in at least one organization, while 27.5% had served as a board chair. They report that they volunteer an average of 12 hours per month for each of these activities, a fairly substantial time commitment.

The types of voluntary involvement display a mixed relationship with the demographic characteristics of the respondents. Types of activities were cross tabulated with demographic characteristics, and Chi Square statistics computed to detect patterns of association. (These results are only suggestive, given the non-random nature of the sample.) A cross-tabulation of voluntary activity types by education and gender categories failed to produce statistically significant Chi Square values. However, the relationship between race and type of activity was significant, with African Americans listing more political activities and more neighborhood-based activities than others. There was also a significant relationship to age, with younger respondents reporting somewhat more social/recreational activities and more human rights activities than the other age groups, and seniors reporting a slightly greater proportion of political and religious activities. Nevertheless, these relationships are generally weak. The more noteworthy finding is how *little* patterns of volunteer involvement appear to vary across the demographic subgroups, within this sample of activists.

Respondents were also asked how they were recruited to each of the organizations they listed. Table 1 groups their responses into broad categories. Verba, Schlozman, and Brady (1995), in their large national survey of civic involvement, found that person-to-person contact ("simply being asked" to use their phrase) was critical to getting people involved. These responses support the importance of direct, personal contact in recruiting people to voluntary organizations in Waterloo/Cedar Falls. Other than self-initiated involvement, various types of personal contact were the most frequent methods by which respondents were recruited.

Most of these contacts appear to involve members or leaders of the organization actively seeking out the person to join, rather than just casual contacts. This suggests that these individuals were already visible in the community and, therefore, considered good recruits for an additional organization. In a number of cases, respondents mentioned that a personal friendship or familial relationship with an existing board member or professional staff member of the organization led to an invitation to become involved, while others described a more formal process of nomination or designation. The following are some typical comments about personal recruitment by others:

- My wife was very involved in ___, so I had lots of [positive] exposure to its programs. Therefore, I said "yes" when asked to volunteer.

- I was approached by the President of the Board, and by another board member.

- I knew the organizers . . .[of the group] . . .I was asked by the director to be on the Board.

- My sister talked me into it, although I was already familiar with the community.

- I knew some of the women involved, and I believed in the mission . . .[of the group.]

TABLE 6.1

How Were You Recruited?		
Organization leader asked	33	22.1%
Volunteered/helped start	27	18.1%
Community leader asked	18	12.1%
Friend asked	15	10.1%
Family influence	13	8.7%
Business associate asked	9	6.0%
Encouraged by training/education	9	6.0%
Political leader appointed	8	5.4%
Mailing/publicity	7	4.7%
Involved in one project	6	4.0%
No response	4	2.7%
Total	149	100.0%

Note: Percentage column may not add up to 100% because of rounding.

Still other comments suggest that self-initiation also played an important role in stimulating involvement, including instances where the respondent actually started the organization:

- I sought out the opportunity because of my desire to help youth.

- I introduced myself, and I volunteered to help keep it [a community center] open longer hours.

- My involvement was self initiated. I have always had an interest in housing issues.

- I initiated the organization . . .[to assist Latino immigrants]. . .I could speak Spanish, and I was inspired by my coursework [Spanish major in college].

To gain a richer picture of participants' involvement, they were asked to describe two organizational projects that they had found particularly satisfying. Respondents most frequently identified projects that involved performing an important task for an organization or achieving some fundamental change within an organization; 52.3% of all projects mentioned fell into these categories. Typical of the organizational change projects reported by respondents were:

- Instituting the nationally recognized "policy governance" model on the board of the local community college.

- Helping to expand a local hospital's heart catheterization and transplant unit.

- Improving administrative procedures at a county facility for the mentally retarded.

- Creating an investment policy for a hospital that satisfied all stakeholders.

These types of projects appeared more frequently than specific programs or fundraisers, suggesting that the respondents valued their ability to make long-term alternations in the course of an organization more than completion of a single activity.

Several participants also mentioned projects to which they contributed unique personal skills: for example, a retired systems analyst who upgraded a non-profit agency's computer system and a banker who helped a non-profit agency make wise investment decisions for its endowment funds. The systems analyst commented: "I support the goals of the ___ organization; it felt good to make their day-to-day operations run more smoothly." The banker commented: "I believe I can do a lot of good in places by guiding their finances. It helps them build a strong base for the organization and its facilities." These responses, along with the data on motivations to be discussed below, suggest the importance of personal empowerment and task accomplishment as sources of satisfaction in both the civic and political realms.

Political Engagement

After describing their volunteer involvement, respondents were asked directly about their political involvement. All were registered to vote, and virtually all had voted in every recent election, including two bond referenda that attracted much lower voter turnouts. Most reported discussing both national and local issues frequently with family and friends. However, most said that they try to avoid strong disagreements over political issues by backing off when opposing views are expressed or by talking mostly to people they agree with. One respondent said she avoided conflict by "hanging out with the right people" while others offered that, since people's minds are already made up, it's not worth the aggravation to debate those holding differing views.

The interview divided political activities beyond voting into two types: seeking to influence particular policy decisions and involvement in election campaigns. All but two of the 40 respondents said they had been involved in trying to influence a public policy decision, while 35 out of 40 said they had been actively involved in trying to elect a particular candidate to office. Activities ranged from phone calls and yard signs to financial contributions and chairing a candidate's local campaign committee. They were more active in local elections than in national elections, and their national election activities were focused on local organizing. Of those who had not participated in campaigns, two cited a professional need to remain politically neutral in public, while the other two cited a dislike of the political process. (A fifth respondent did not answer this question.) An African-American woman said of her non-involvement, "I'm just not a politics girl." For most of these community activists, however, political activity appears to be an important part of their community involvement, along with participation in private, voluntary organizations. This additional evidence further undermines Proposition 1, in that respondents appear to move comfortably across the boundary between civic and political engagement.

Sources of Satisfaction and Dissatisfaction

Another way to examine the boundary between the civic and the political is to contrast the attitudes and experiences of the respondents as they participated in both realms. This attitudinal dimension is reflected in Proposition 2. An important set of attitudes associated with both civic and political involvement consists of the satisfactions and frustrations experienced by participants, because these will either attract or repel them when they consider new or continuing participatory opportunities. If the psychological reward structure for civic involvement is substantially different than that for political involvement, then this suggests a clear experiential boundary between the two, even though most community activists cross this boundary regularly. In Tables 2 and 3, the open-ended responses to these questions have been categorized so that the contrasts

TABLE 6.2 | *Sources of Satisfaction and Obstacles in Volunteer Projects*

Sources of satisfaction (What made this activity or project particularly satisfying for you?)			Obstacles (What obstacles or difficulties did you encounter?)		
Accomplishment of goal	28	32.9%	Opposition from key actors	13	16.7%
Personal relationships (coworkers & recipients)	16	18.8%	Low level of participation, volunteering	9	11.5%
Skill acquisition or utilization	12	14.1%	Resistance by recipients	8	10.3%
Satisfaction of problem solving	6	7.1%	Lack of time	7	9.0%
Helping children/youth	5	5.9%	Competition/turf issues	6	7.7%
Group representation/ empowerment	5	5.9%	Other	6	7.7%
Giving back to community	3	3.5%	No major obstacles	5	6.4%
Positive feedback from recipients	3	3.5%	Lack of funding	5	6.4%
General community benefit	3	3.5%	Conflict among participants	5	6.4%
Personal empathy with recipients	2	2.4%	Coordination	5	6.4%
Positive feedback on performance	1	1.2%	Getting/keeping motivated people	3	3.8%
Helping those in need	1	1.2%	Lack of knowledge of procedures	2	2.6%
	85	100.0%	Lack of professional staff support	2	2.6%
			Hassles from public bureaucracies	2	2.6%
				78	100.0%

Note: Respondents could list up to two specific volunteer projects that they worked on and many listed more than one source of satisfaction or dissatisfaction for each project. These data are based on 85 responses given by the 40 respondents to these questions. Columns may not add up to 100% due to rounding.

between the two realms can be shown clearly. Table 2 displays the sources of satisfaction and frustration respondents encountered in their civic activities, while Table 3 reports their satisfactions and dissatisfactions from participating in political activities.

In comparing the distribution of responses in these two tables, one first notices that these activists are very goal oriented in *both* their volunteer activities and their political activities. In the case of volunteer activities, accomplishment of the goal is most frequently listed as the major source of satisfaction, while in political campaigning, electing a candidate who reflects one's policy preferences (i.e., achieving one's policy goals) is the most frequently cited source of satisfaction. A senior white female reported working hard within her religious denomination to gain recognition and empowerment for Native American members and she cited as her major source of satisfaction, "getting it done after putting in so much work on the issue." In the case of campaigning, the following statements about sources of satisfaction were typical responses:

- Working for a candidate you believe in, who can make a difference.

- It is a way to influence public policy.

- The candidate has integrity, confidence. It was time for a change.

- I believed in the candidate's message.

Conversely, having one's candidate lose is listed as the most important source of frustration, and opposition from key actors is cited as the most important frustration with volunteer activities. A respondent who had

TABLE 6.3 | *Sources of Satisfaction and Dissatisfaction with Campaign Involvement*

Sources of satisfaction in campaigning (What were the most satisfying aspects of working for this candidate's campaign?)			Sources of dissatisfaction in campaigning (What were the least satisfying aspects of working for this candidate's campaign?)		
Agreement with candidate on public policy	10	28.6%	Having candidate lose	10	28.6%
Admiration for personal qualities of candidate	7	20.0%	Personal interactions uncomfortable	8	22.9%
Personal interactions	4	11.4%	Negative/misleading/partisan campaign	5	14.3%
Feeling of making a difference	4	11.4%	Time consuming	3	8.6%
Educating citizens on political issues	4	11.4%	Apathy of voters	3	8.6%
Learning organizational skills	2	5.7%	Issues or points of view ignored, diluted	3	8.6%
Gaining representation for an excluded group	2	5.7%	Nature of campaign work	1	2.9%
No satisfaction	1	2.9%	Poor choices of candidates	1	2.9%
No response	1	2.9%	No response	1	2.9%
	35	100.0%		35	100.0%

Note: Respondents were asked about their general sources of satisfaction and dissatisfaction with campaign activities. Only one response was recorded for each question. Five respondents did not participate in campaign activities. Columns may not add up to 100% due to rounding.

worked on a hospital project found the opposition from other hospitals in town frustrating, stating that they "didn't believe__Hospital's financial statements and thought the hospital should close down, rather than expand." Another respondent complained in more general terms of "persons in authority who control money and put up hurdles." With regard to political activity, several respondents expressed their frustration in phrases, such as "seeing [the candidate] lose after all that time spent," suggesting that they may be questioning the wisdom of have invested so much time for so little result. An important difference between volunteer and electoral activities is that the former tend to be ongoing, while the latter are competitions that end at a specific time and produce a winner and a loser. For a goal-oriented person, the prospect of wasting one's effort by backing a loser can potentially be a deterrent to choosing political involvement over volunteer efforts.

A second point of comparison is the greater importance of personal relationships in volunteering, as opposed to electoral activity. In Table 2, the category "Personal relationships" is second only to goal achievement in its frequency as a source of satisfaction from these activists' volunteer experiences. This includes relationships with the recipients of the service, as well as with other volunteers. In addition, personal identification or empathy with recipients is an important source of satisfaction for some respondents. For example, one woman stated that "I gained particular satisfaction from helping children avoid or report child abuse because I was abused myself as a child." All of these factors point to the personal nature of volunteering.

In contrast, the distribution of responses in Table 3 suggests that respondents view political campaigning as a more strictly instrumental activity. Only two respondents mentioned personal interactions during campaigns as a source of satisfaction, and two others expressed discomfort with the kind of interactions that campaigns required of them. (One specifically mentioned her dislike of calling up strangers to ask for their support.) This does not mean that personal relationships are not an important part of a political campaign, but rather that they are not a central source of satisfaction. Even though these activists were willing to cross the boundary into politics, the characteristics of campaigning that they note could deter less motivated folk.

A somewhat surprising finding is that respondents mentioned the non-participation of others as a source of dissatisfaction more frequently in their volunteer activities than in their political activities. Given the well-documented political apathy of most American citizens, one would expect this to be a source of frustration among those who try to mobilize them to vote. However, in a campaign, one's coworkers are usually well motivated, and one works alongside them to move the mass of citizenry to the polls. If the masses stay away in droves, it is frustrating but it does not necessarily impose a heavier work burden on volunteers.

In contrast, volunteer activity requires direct commitment of time and energy by citizens in order to be completed, and it counts success, in part, by the number of people directly served. Therefore, if only a few volunteers show up, it puts an undue work burden on those who do, and if clients do not show, it makes the whole effort seem futile. Both of these outcomes led to considerable frustration on the part of the respondents. One respondent complained about "capable people who don't give their time." Another complained that "people show up for a hot issue and then leave." Many pointed out that when groups have to rely on the same small group of people again and again, those people feel over-extended and can burn out. They also understandably believe that volunteer efforts would be a lot more successful in reaching their goals if more citizens would, as one respondent put it, "carry their weight and follow through on promises."

Responses to questions about sources of satisfaction and dissatisfaction thus lend support to Proposition 2; that the political and civic realms of community activity are somewhat distinct in the rewards and frustrations that they present. Activists view them as different arenas, at the same time that most are involved in both. These responses also lend support to Proposition 5; that those who are involved hold very negative opinions of those who are not.

Participation as a Learning Process

The civic engagement literature views citizen involvement as a process by which citizens acquire new skills, develop self confidence, learn to manage conflict, and broaden their perspectives on the world. In contrast. Eliasoph observed that participants were learning negative attitudes that constrained the nature and breadth of their involvement. To assess the developmental aspect of participation for these activists, they were asked what they had learned from their civic engagement experiences. Table 4, in which the open-ended responses to this question are placed into broad categories, displays a quite diverse array of learning experiences.

The most frequent theme was that of personal empowerment. Respondents conveyed the sense that participation teaches personal efficacy and confidence, lessons that can be carried forward to the next experience. One woman stated, "I was able to overcome a feeling of inferiority working with state experts. I found that I knew as much as most of the people on the committee." Another mentioned that her volunteer experience had "increased her confidence in her leadership abilities." A third stated that "I am no longer apologetic about asking for money."

The next most frequently mentioned categories of learning involved enhancement of interpersonal skills. Patience and tolerance were the most frequently mentioned skills, but a variety of other interpersonal skills were also highlighted. An African-American male said he had learned that "patience in stressful situations can produce common ground." The importance of teamwork was also mentioned by several. A neighborhood leader said she had learned "the power of banding together in a coalition. People will listen." In addition to these "getting along" skills, respondents mentioned the value of persistence and intense commitment. As one African-American respondents stated it, "Persistence pays off. Stay with your dream." Several respondents also came away with a heightened awareness of the importance of power and competition for resources in trying

TABLE 6.4 | *Learning from Participation*

What did you learn from this activity? Did it change you in any way as a person?		
Personal empowerment	16	17.2%
Persistence	14	15.1%
Enhanced personal skills	13	14.0%
Patience and tolerance	12	12.9%
Understanding of process	5	5.4%
New respect for recipients	5	5.4%
Importance of teamwork	4	4.3%
Conflict with "powers" inevitable	3	3.2%
Strengthened commitment to cause	3	3.2%
People will help	3	3.2%
Public attitudes fixed, hard to change	3	3.2%
Strength in numbers	2	2.1%
Importance of history	2	2.1%
Competition for resources	2	2.1%
Need to pull in new volunteers, not same ones	2	2.1%
Need clear, even provocative message	2	2.1%
Important to celebrate successes	1	1.1%
Broadened contacts in community	1	1.1%
	93	100.0%

Note: Percentage column may not add up to 100% due to rounding.

to achieve community goals. *Not* included in their responses was any sense of their having learned to avoid "politics" and stick to strictly non-political projects.

In examining these responses, one must keep in mind that most of these respondents were already seasoned community activists before they took on the projects documented in the interviews. What they cited as "learning" may, therefore, have been reinforcement of previously held beliefs. However, whether or not learning involves reinforcing old ideas or acquiring genuinely new insights, these responses suggest the value of ongoing civic participation in building a repertoire of skills and understandings that can subsequently be applied to new projects. They also do not reveal the patterns of anti-political learning suggested by Eliasoph.

To assess what respondents had learned from their experiences in the political process, the interviews asked what factors they believed had contributed to the success or failure of their efforts to influence policy. The responses of those who considered they had succeeded are categorized in Table 5. Whereas respondents' comments on civic engagement stressed the interpersonal skills of working with others within an organized group, their comments about their attempts to influence public policy stressed the presence or absence of effective communication with, and education of, decision makers and the public as a critical factor in success. One respondent commented on a successful effort that "we did a good job with the education. . .[of decision-makers]. Our lobbyists were knowledgeable and our members were kept informed." Another stated that "we were well organized, and we were able to communicate the importance of research on diabetes to decision-makers." Respondents also stressed as a critical factor the intensity of motivation of the citizens backing the project.

While one must be cautious in inferring too much from a limited set of responses, it seems clear that the respondents view themselves as "girding for battle" when they enter the public policy arena, rather than engaging in a collective, cooperative project as they do in the civic engagement arena. They want highly motivated "troops" who can deliver their message effectively to whoever makes the decisions. It is not that they fail to

TABLE 6.5 | *Reasons for Success in Influencing Policy*

(Why do you consider your efforts to influence government decisions to have been a success?)		
Quality of organization/networking	13	25.5%
Receptivity of decision makers	10	19.6%
Effective education or publicity	7	13.7%
Staying focused, on message	3	5.9%
Financial resources	3	5.9%
Persistence	3	5.9%
Level of public's interest	3	5.9%
Information provided	2	3.9%
Motivation of participants	2	3.9%
Putting a human face on problem	2	3.9%
Numbers of supporters	1	2.0%
Validity of cause	1	2.0%
Positive approach	1	2.0%
	51	100.0%

Note: Percentage column may not add up to 100% due to rounding.

mention conflict in their discussion of civic projects. Rather, the need to state one's case forcefully is more central to political action. These perceptions of the difference between civic and political engagement do not deter these activists from fighting for the policy outcomes they desire. However, these responses raise the possibility that other less committed citizens may be turned off by this element of conflict in the political process.

How to Mobilize Others

The data presented so far have shown the willingness of community activists to participate both in community service activities and in the policy and electoral aspects of politics. Their comments reflect awareness that these arenas contain different obstacles and different sources of satisfaction. At the same time, they are very goal oriented in both arenas, and they recognize the need to effectively mobilize new participants in both arenas. Therefore, the next step in this analysis is to examine how these activists view the process of mobilizing other citizens to participate in both civic and political activities. The responses of these activists reveal a painful awareness that large percentages of the public participate neither in volunteer service activities nor in the political process. The question is how to *motivate* more citizens to become active.

A reasonable place to begin figuring out how to motivate others is to examine one's own motivations for participation. Respondents were very self-aware and thoughtful about their own reasons for participating,

TABLE 6.6 | *Motivations for Participation*

Motivations for own activity (What is your primary motivation for involvement?)		
To give back to the community that has nurtured you	11	20.0%
Personal empowerment	9	16.4%
Service to those less privileged	8	14.5%
To improve the community	6	10.9%
Citizen's obligation to participate in process	6	10.9%
Self improvement	5	9.1%
Modeling by family or community of origin	4	7.3%
	4	7.3%
Obligation to future generations	2	3.6%
	55	100.0%
Motivations for others to be active (Why do you think it is important for people [in general] to be involved?)		
Involvement is empowering	14	31.8%
Each person has an obligation to serve, to "give back"	13	29.5%
Self improvement	10	22.7%
Critical community tasks won't get done	4	9.1%
Each person has unique gifts to offer	3	6.8%
	44	100.0%

Note: Percentage columns may not add up to 100% due to rounding.

providing quite detailed answers. Therefore, the analysis of how to motivate others should begin by examining what these activists said about their own motivations. Earlier questions asked about motivations for specific political and non-political projects. In the questions analyzed here, respondents were first asked to reflect on their overall experience with community activism, both in volunteerism and in political action, and to discuss their own motivations for being active in the community. Their open-ended responses are summarized in Table 6. Respondents were then asked to discuss their main sources of frustration with their involvement and what inspires them to keep going in the face of these frustrations. Responses to this question are categorized and summarized in Table 7.

In these responses, as in the earlier responses concerning specific projects, a strong belief in reciprocity emerges as the primary motive for involvement. The community is viewed as having conferred benefits on the individual and, as a result, the individual has an obligation to "give back" by trying to make the community better. James Coleman, in his original formulation of the idea of social capital, emphasized the notion of mutual expectations of support as a critical element in social capital linkages between people (Coleman, 1988). For these respondents, however, it is not a specific obligation to pay back a particular individual, but rather an obligation to the entire community that drives their participation. As one senior white male expressed it, "I have a duty as member of the community to enhance it and improve the quality of life. Everyone should contribute because all of us are smarter than any one of us."

Other respondents specifically mentioned an obligation to help the less fortunate, citing the duty of those with privilege to help those without it. A young white woman who had been raised in a single parent home said,

TABLE 6.7 | *Sources of Frustration and Perseverance in Community Involvement*

General sources of frustration with involvement (What frustrates you the most being involved in the community?)			What keeps you going when things get ? frustrating		
Lack of commitment/involvement by others	19	47.5%	Strong personal commitment to involvement	15	28.3%
Time constraints; competing demands of work, family	7	17.5%	Taking a longer term, "big picture" perspective	9	17.0%
Conflict or lack of cooperation	6	15.0%	Seeing positive results of actions	7	13.2%
				7	13.2%
Slowness of progress on issues	4	10.0%	Personal religious faith	6	11.4%
Lack of funds	2	5.0%	Support from others	5	9.4%
Arrogance or unresponsiveness of leaders	2	5.0%	Take a break; step back for awhile	4	7.5%
	40	100.0%	Personal empowerment	4	7.5%
			Staying hopeful about future	1	1.9%
			Flexibility—change projects if one not working	1	1.9%
			Tolerance and love for others	1	1.9%
				53	100.0%

Note: Respondents were asked for the single most frustrating thing about involvement. They could give more than one response on factors that kept them motivated.

"I am motivated by a desire to change things for the better—social justice. There was no particular event that first caused my involvement, but rather a mentality and belief that I should be on the side of the underdog." Another stated that she is motivated by the desire "to learn to help offer opportunities to those without them."

A second common theme is that of personal empowerment. Respondents like the feeling that they can really "make a difference" in the community. One respondent stated his motivation as "the desire to contribute to positive change" while another wished to "do something to make a difference and provide leadership." While these motives might appear egocentric at first glance, Robert Wuthnow (1991) reminds us that altruism always has a strong component of satisfying personal needs within it, and that this does not negate the significance or moral validity of the urge to help others. Instead, the notion of empowerment through helping others represents an enlargement of one's sense of self to include the well-being of others as essential to one's own. This conclusion also applies to the theme of personal growth and development that is stressed by a number of respondents. A young white male cited "the reward you get yourself" as a motivation and went on to say that involvement "builds self esteem." An African-American male stated that "It is personally satisfying to see results, plus involvement builds contacts and skills."

The lack of participation by others is the most frequently mentioned source of frustration for these respondents. Several mentioned with disfavor "those that could help, but don't" or "those that come out for one issue and then disappear." One respondent expressed his frustration in the following way: "The number of participants is always small. Most people don't know how to become involved, and then they lack time to spend on the community because they are struggling to make ends meet." Two other themes mentioned by several respondents were their frustration at the slow progress made on some issues and at the personal time constraints they face, as they try to balance their activism with work and family obligations. Interestingly, lack of funding was not mentioned as frequently as the human interactions involved in participation, even though it is common for programs of social improvement to operate under severe funding constraints.

Another way of tapping underlying motives is to ask what keeps people going in the face of frustrations. The most frequently cited source of inspiration was their own deep, personal commitment to be involved. Numerous comments by respondents convey the sense that they derive a deep, ethical satisfaction from engagement that transcends short-term frustrations. Their next most frequent method of coping with frustration was to take a longer term view of things as a way of lessening the sting of short-term setbacks. Several respondents used phrases like "things go in cycles" or "what goes around, comes around" to express their feeling that defeat or discouragement at one point in time will not necessarily be permanent. Finally, respondents were able to rely on the support of others who appreciate their efforts and on their satisfaction at what they *had* accomplished to buoy them up in the face of difficulties. Several said that one should "celebrate small victories" and keep moving ahead.

Because of the recent attention given to faith-based initiatives, special note should be taken of the role of religious faith as a motivator for these respondents (Wuthnow, 1999). Almost all of them were asked how important religious faith was as a motivation for community action. (A few were not, because this question was not included in an initial version of the interview protocol.) Over two-thirds (68.0%)said that their faith was a very important or somewhat important motivation for their involvement. However, they did not approve of expressing one's faith in a way that would try to preach to others or to impose one's beliefs on them. They believe that their faith is best expressed through their actions toward the community. (The quote at the beginning of this essay expresses this view eloquently.) This is very similar to the perspective on religious faith that this author found in an earlier study of Habitat for Humanity volunteers (Hays 2002).

Even though respondents were very thoughtful about their own motivations for involvement, most of them struggled with the question of why others do not get involved and how to motivate more people to get involved. Table 8 groups into broad categories the reasons why respondents believe that voting has declined in recent years and their proffered solutions to this problem. This table also presents the reasons why respondents believe that it is hard to get people involved in the local community, along with the solutions that they propose.

Citizens' fatalism and apathy top the lists of reasons for both non-voting and lack of local participation. The most common phrase was "people don't think it will make a difference." At worst, this explanation is tautological, in that it accounts for non-participation by apathy when really "apathy" is just another way of

TABLE 6.8 | *Reasons for Lack of Voting and Local Citizen Involvement*

Why is voting on the decline?			Why is it hard to get local involvement?		
Individual Attributes		**46.3%**	**Individual Attributes**		**61.2%**
Fatalism; sense of powerlessness	12	17.9%	Only concerned with issues immediately affecting them	14	20.9%
Citizen's lack of knowledge of complex issues	10	14.9%			
			Apathy, fatalism, complacency	11	16.4%
Lack of civic responsibility	9	13.4%	Don't understand the true impact of local decisions	9	13.4%
			Dislike conflict	5	7.5%
			Don't understand how the system works	2	3.0%
Attributes of leaders or political system		**43.3%**	**Attributes of leaders or political system**		**13.4%**
Distrust of politicians and political process	9	13.4%	Leaders are unresponsive	5	7.5%
Politicians do not communicate with voters effectively	5	7.5%	Lack of media attention to local issues	3	4.5%
Country divided/values changing	5	7.5%	Not asked to be involved	1	1.5%
Citizens can't see clear party or candidate differences	4	6.0%			
Influence of money negates citizen influence	3	4.5%			
Media don't focus on important issues	3	4.5%			
Mixed Attributes		**10.5%**	**Mixed Attributes**		**25.4%**
Lack of time/competing interests	4	6.0%	Time constraints; competing demands of work, family	17	25.4%
Other	3	4.5%			
Total	**67**	**100.0%**	**Total**	**67**	**100.0%**

Note: Rounding error may result in column percentages summing slightly above or below accurate totals.

stating non-participation At best, this view explains non-participation as rooted in some psychological disposition that individuals innately possess, rather than in a situational analysis of why they might not care. It is analogous to "explaining" why someone doesn't eat chocolate ice cream by saying "She doesn't like it." Respondents are clearly viewing most citizens as less motivated than they are, but they are not probing below the surface to ask why this lack of motivation exists.

As their second and third most frequent responses to lack of voting, respondents do offer some causal explanations for non-involvement; namely, lack of voter knowledge and education, and lack of responsiveness or effective communication by political leaders. These responses point beyond individual predispositions and

TABLE 6.9 | *How to Improve Electoral and Local Participation*

How to improve electoral turnout			How to improve local involvement		
Education		**34.6%**	**Education**		**50.0%**
Voter registration and education efforts	9	17.3%	Educate adults on importance of issues	9	18.0%
Civic education of youth	8	15.4%	Educate youth	6	12.0%
Civic education of adults	1	1.9%	Encourage people to see beyond self	5	10.0%
			Change by example or by direct experience	5	10.0%
Changes in Political System		**48.1%**	**Outreach by those 'In System'**		**50.0%**
Candidates encourage involvement; connect with voters	6	11.5%	Personal invitation and outreach by those involved	14	28.0%
Those already involved reach out to uninvolved	5	9.6%	More respect for diverse individual and group perspectives	3	6.0%
Elect officials who command respect and trust	4	7.7%	Strong, clear, positive messages from leaders	3	6.0%
Make the voting process easier	3	5.8%	Better media coverage and message	3	6.0%
Create opportunities for successful involvement	3	5.8%	Leaders more receptive to citizen input	1	2.0%
Media improve issue coverage	2	3.8%	Focus on retirees	1	2.0%
Campaign finance reform	2	3.8%			
Other		**17.3%**	**Total**	**50**	**100.0%**
Citizens should seek out appropriate involvement	1	1.9%			
Seek out successful models of involvement	1	1.9%			
Limit the vote to property owners	1	1.9%			
Use slander laws to punish negative campaigning	1	1.9%			
Miscellaneous	3	5.8%			
Don't know	2	3.8%			
Total	**52**	**100.0%**			

Note: Rounding error may result in column percentages summing slightly above or below accurate totals.

towards systemic reasons why citizens might not be coming forward. However, again, respondents are not specific about what is wrong with leaders' communication, nor do they suggest in what way citizens or youth should be educated. They also do not consider that education alone is unlikely to be effective in inducing participation, unless there are structured opportunities to utilize this learning. Like many other subjects people are exposed to in school, civic education will be forgotten if it is not later utilized.

Table 9 shows that respondents' suggestions for improving electoral turnout differ from their suggestions for improving local participation. For the former, they most frequently list general voter outreach and education as a solution, followed by civic education, and better communication by candidates. No one group or institution is given the primary responsibility for doing this, although many activists single out the media by contrasting what they perceive as its currently negative effect on participation with its potential to genuinely educate citizens. In this, they support Putnam's view that electronic media are toxic to civic engagement (Putnam, 2000).

Their suggestions for increasing *local* involvement attribute a greater degree of agency to local activists by stressing personal outreach and invitation to participate on the part of those already involved. Reflecting the more personal, face-to-face character of local involvement, they believe that one-on-one outreach and role modeling by those already involved can be an effective way to mobilize non-participants. For example, one white female retiree, who has been active in her religious denomination's social concerns committee, suggests finding projects involving short-term commitments that get people "hooked" and then gradually drawing them into the network of activists. However, in addition to this personal outreach, respondents place considerable weight on civic education and a community that is receptive to diverse outlooks. Here, as in the case of voting, they are willing to put responsibility on the community to foster participation, rather than just leaving it to the individual to form the will to get involved.

Taken together, these responses about mobilizing other citizens lend support to Proposition 5, that there is a large gap between how activists perceive themselves and how they perceive those who are not active. Activists direct a considerable amount of frustration and negativity at non-participants, and many of them lack a clear idea of how to bridge the gap and mobilize others. As one respondent put it, "When you find out. . .[how to get people involved]. . .let me know!"

CONCLUSIONS

The analysis presented in this case study suggests that persons active in the local community do perceive a boundary between engagement in voluntary, civic activities, and political participation. They view politics as an arena of advocacy and, frequently, conflict, while they stress working together and cooperation in their civic endeavors. The satisfactions they derive from involvement in politics derive from the successful promotion of fairly abstract policy outcomes, whether through electing a candidate or through lobbying on an issue. In contrast, they see volunteer activity much more as an opportunity for personal growth and satisfying interactions with others, although they are also very goal oriented in these activities, and they frequently mention the presence of conflict and competition here, as well as in political activities.

Nevertheless, almost all of these individuals have crossed the boundary between civic involvement and political participation, as they have been actively engaged in both arenas. One does not get from their responses any sense of the barriers to political action that Eliasoph suggests are put up by organizations engaged in civic activities. Their willingness to move from one form of involvement to the other, and their view that both are part of the citizen's obligation to the community, support Putnam's idea that civic and political engagement are closely linked.

At the same time, their responses suggest that strong barriers to both civic and political participation remain among the majority of the population that is not involved in either. Activists view the typical citizen as alienated from the community, both in terms of knowledge about what is really going on and in terms of an emotional rejection of the value of becoming involved. What is perhaps more significant is that activists do not seem to have any clear idea as to what might overcome these barriers. Their responses reveal considerable reflection on their own motivations, but they become vague and tautological when discussing what should be done to motivate others.

Because all citizens are deeply embedded in current institutions and practices, it is difficult for them to see the barriers to participation that are built into the political economy of American urban communities. As suggested by Putnam and other advocates for renewed civic engagement, the economic system fuels its own expansion by fostering rampant consumerism, which, in turn, contributes to the isolation of individuals and ...wn private worlds. Despite their frequently expressed pieties about the need to participate, ...motivation to genuinely involve the large mass of citizenry because any expansion of ...predictable consequences for those currently in power (Schattschneider, 1960). ...itical systems are oriented to giving ordinary citizens an active voice, other than ...nd carefully structured alternatives at the ballot box (Crenson & Ginsberg, 2002). ...o do get more actively involved quickly learn the importance of involvement and also the capacity of involved citizens to occasionally achieve meaningful results. However, they remain permanently frustrated by their inability to pull a larger percentage of the population into the civic and political arena, as well as very unclear as to what obstacles they are really up against.

Therefore, the boundaries between no involvement and civic involvement and between civic involvement and political involvement remain porous only to a few. Activists can make these leaps, but they pull others with them on an infrequent basis. Here is where Eliasoph is on target. Political systems in most urban communities have not fostered a dialogue among all citizens, both active and inactive, as to how to create "public spaces" that encourage meaningful political connections and meaningful political action on the part of ordinary citizens. A society that created such spaces would be very different from the one we currently experience, even though huge concentrations of economic and political power would still constrain citizen action. A much wider range of needs and viewpoints would be on the table, and institutions would be encouraged to be responsive to more than just the powerful few.

REFERENCES

Barber, B. R. (1998). *A place for us: How to make society civil and democracy strong.* New York: Hill and Wang.

Bellah, R. (1985). *Habits of the heart: Individualism and commitment in American life.* Berkley: University of California Press.

Berry, J. M. (1999). The rise of citizen groups. In Theda Skocpol & Morris P. Fiorina (Eds.), *Civic engagement in American democracy* (pp. 367–394). Washington and New York: Brookings and Russell Sage.

Berry, J. M., Portney, K. E., & Thompson, K. (1993). *The rebirth of urban democracy.* Washington, DC: The Brookings Institution.

Casamayou, M. (2002). Collective entrepreneurialism and breast cancer advocacy. In Allan J. Cigler & Burdett A. Loomis (Eds.), *Interest group politics,* 6th Ed. (pp. 79–95). Washington, DC: CQ Press.

Coleman, J. S. (1988). Social capital in the creation of human capital. *American Journal of Sociology,* 94, S95–S120.

Crenson, M.A., & Ginsberg, B. (2002). *Downsizing democracy: How America sidelined its citizens and privatized its public.* Baltimore: Johns Hopkins University Press.

Edwards, B., & Foley, M. W. (1997). Social capital and the political economy of our discontent. *American Behavioral Scientist,* 40(5), 669–678.

Eliasoph, N. (1998). *Avoiding politics: How Americans produce apathy in everyday life.* New York: Cambridge University Press.

Ericson, R. S., & Tedin, K. L. (2003). *American public opinion: Its origins, content and impact.* Sixth Ed. New York: Longman.

Etzioni, A. (Ed.) (1998). *The essential communitarian reader.* New York: Rowman and Littlefield.

Hays, R. A. (2002). Habitat for Humanity: Building social capital through faith based service. *Journal of Urban Affairs,* 24(3), 247–269.

Hooghe, M., & Stolle, D. (Eds.) (2003). *Generating social capital: Civil society and institutions in comparative perspective.* New York: Palgrave.

Lin, N. (2001). *Social capital: A theory of social structure and action.* Cambridge, UK: Cambridge University Press.

Putnam, R. D. (1993). *Making democracy work: Civic traditions in modern Italy.* Princeton, NJ: Princeton University Press.

Putnam, R. D. (1995). Bowling alone: America's declining social capital. *Journal of Democracy,* 6(1), 65–78.

Putnam, R. D. (2000). *Bowling alone: The collapse and revival of American community.* New York: Simon and Schuster.

Schattschneider, E. E. (1960). *The semi-sovereign people: A realist's view of democracy in America.* New York: Holt.

Skocpol, T. (1996). Unravelling from above. *The American Prospect,* 25, 20–25.

Skocpol, T. (2000). *The missing middle: Working families and the future of American social policy.* New York: W.W. Norton.

Skocpol, T., & Fiorina, M.P. (Eds.) (1999). *Civic engagement in American democracy.* Washington, DC: Brookings Institution.

Stolle, D. (2000). *Communities of trust: Social capital and public action in comparative perspective.* Ph.D. dissertation. Princeton University.

Stone, C. N. (1989). *Regime politics: Governing Atlanta*, 1946–1988. Lawrence: University Press of Kansas.

Verba, S., Schlozman, K.L., & Brady, H. E. (1995). *Voice and equality: Civic voluntarism in American politics.* Cambridge, MA: Harvard University Press.

Woolcock, M. (1998). Social capital and economic development: Toward a theoretical synthesis and policy framework. *Theory and Society*, 27(2), 151–208.

Woolcock, M., & Narayan, D. (2000). Social capital: Implications for development theory, research and policy. *World Bank Research Observer*, 15(2), 225–249.

Wuthnow, R. (1991). *Acts of compassion: Caring for others and helping ourselves.* Princeton, NJ: Princeton University Press.

Wuthnow, R. (1999). Mobilizing civic engagement: The changing impact of religious involvement. In Theda Skocpol & Morris P. Fiorina (Eds.), *Civic engagement in American democracy* (pp. 331–366). Washington, DC: Brookings Institution.

Yates, D. (1980). *The ungovernable city: The politics of urban problems and policy making.* Cambridge, MA:MIT Press.

Yin, R. K. (1994). *Case study research: Design and methods*, 2nd Ed. Thousand Oaks, CA: Sage Publications.

1. Civic engagement is [obscured] paragraph, describe how you [obscured] a community organization is helping you develop knowledge and skills that are useful to a citizen.

2. Briefly describe the four "zones of engagement" in your own life. Do you feel that the experience of being a volunteer helps you to cross the boundary from the Civic Engagement zone to the Political Engagement zone? Why or why not?

3. There are three types of organizations in the Civic Engagement zone. How would you describe the organization in which you are a volunteer? In talking with others in the organization, do they move from the Civic Engagement zone to the Political Engagement zone? Or, do the people in the organization tend to remain within a single zone? Do you find any attitudinal barriers that make boundary crossing difficult?

4. Describe how you and others who are part of the organization in which you are a volunteer confirm (or refute) any two or more of Hays' five propositions about the boundaries between the Civic Engagement and the Political Engagement zones.

5. Are there significant differences between the social setting of Hays' research in an Iowa city and your locality? How might these differences affect what you experience in observing the boundaries between the zones in the organization in which you are a volunteer?

7 PARTICIPATING AS A CITIZEN IN YOUR COMMUNITY

—Jim Watkins and Harvey K. Newman

Which of the following situations involves politics? Which involves power?

1. As a recent college graduate you want your parent to cosign a note so that you can buy a brand new car.

2. Your colleague at work with whom you share workspace is a wonderful person to work with except for his messiness which has now spilled over into your workspace.

3. For the third time in a week, your next door neighbor's dog has gotten loose and chased your cat up a tree.

4. The local school board is voting next week on which science curriculum will be taught.

5. Your nonprofit group is trying to get a zoning variance so that it can expand parking.

6. A committee of the state legislature is deciding whether or not to reduce the state budget deficit by cutting Medicaid payments to nursing homes.

7. Congress and the administration are investigating options to health care reform.

Politics and power are much maligned and much misunderstood. All the above involve politics and power.

Politics is simply the way people relate to one another to accomplish something. There is politics in our families, schools, neighborhoods, workplaces city councils, and even in our nonprofit organizations. All of us are pretty good politicians. We know how to relate to others in order to get what we want. Power is the ability to do a particular thing. Look again at the situations described above. Who has the power to cosign, clean up the work area, control the dog, choose a curriculum, get a variance, decide on Medicaid payments, or develop a national health care policy? Power moves, and people who have power to accomplish something in one arena may not have power in another arena. For example, the local school board does not have the power to decide whether your coworker cleans up his messy workspace. Like politics, power is involved in all our relationships.

What most people call politics is the public policy process. The public policy process places politics and power, which operate in all human arenas, into the public square where decisions are made for the public good. The public policy process is the way society sets community norms, often through law. What will we teach in our schools? What will our infrastructure (roads, bridges, rail, etc.) look like? What kind of health care will be available, particularly for the uninsured, especially the disabled and children? Power and politics are involved in all the situations listed above. Situations one and two do not involve the public policy process; situations four, five, six, and seven do involve the public policy process. Situation three could involve the public policy process if your community has a leash law.

Another way of looking at the relationship of politics, power, and the public policy process is to think about the types of activities in which an individual citizen can participate in a nonprofit as a volunteer. Obviously nonprofit organizations use the time and energy of their volunteers in a variety of ways in order to provide services. As Table One shows there are several ways in which individual citizens can participate to make change in their communities.

The first type of individual activity in which citizens engage is one to one. Citizens who serve as volunteers often engage an issue or community need on a one-to-one basis such as serving one night a week in a soup kitchen and befriending a homeless man. This activity improves direct service to people in need, but has little impact on changing community norms.

The second option is for citizens who serve as volunteers to create options to a system. An example might be a group that decides to build several homes for those in need of affordable housing. This improves direct service and promotes some system change because there are now options available that did not exist before. However, community norms and root causes are still not directly addressed. There will be no long-term change in the system.

Next on the list is for volunteers to monitor the system. Monitoring means being present when public policy decisions (community norms for community good) are made and administered and asking questions. "Why?" "What is going on?" An example might be going to the county commission and inquiring about plans for providing affordable housing in the county. This activity provides less direct service than serving in a soup kitchen, but has a greater potential for system change as community norms, root causes, and the concept of the common good are addressed in the public square. Volunteers can also work for good public policy through advocating for particular legislation. As people use their time and energy to be involved in the public square helping to form legislation for the public good, they may provide less direct service. However, as community norms are changed for the better, as laws are made and enacted, there will be system change. Root causes of

TABLE 7.1

Type of Activity	Impact on Direct Service	Impact on System Change
1. One to one	A little improvement in direct service	Little if any system change
2. Create options to system	A bit more improvement in direct service	A little bit more potential for system change
3. Monitor system (be present & ask questions)	Less direct service	More potential for system change
4. Relating to government (public policy advocacy)	Less direct service	More potential for system change
5. Confront system	Less direct service	More potential for system change

human need will be addressed. For example, how do our laws and ordinances embody incentives for building affordable housing?

Finally, volunteers can confront systems in the public square. This does not mean violence. It does mean turning on the spotlight of public opinion. Sometimes, as in the civil rights movement, this activity has the greatest potential for system change. A story on the six o'clock news about the lack of affordable housing helps change the system.

These different ways of volunteering are not mutually exclusive. One way is not better than another. The table describes how people volunteer in various ways and what impact their activity has on changing systems that impact the lives of others. People often move back and forth along the continuum according to interest and talents. There are many ways in which to be a good volunteer. However, any in-depth engagement as a volunteer should lead you to ask questions about the common good in the public square where power is used through politics.

Where are most people in nonprofit agencies who volunteer their time? Most are engaged in one-to-one activity or in creating options to a system. Again, this is not good or bad; right or wrong. One of the tasks of bridging the gap between the civic and the political arenas is to recognize that people can move along the continuum of activities. People who have served in soup kitchens for years and wonder why the lines stay so long can be more effective if they examine their community's provision for low- and moderate-income housing. Volunteers who have worked on housing issues at city hall for years can serve in a soup line every now and then so that the policy they work on has a face.

As persons move from one-to-one and group involvement to monitoring, public policy advocacy and confrontation, it is important to reflect on why you (and others) serve as volunteers. What do you get out of serving as a volunteer? How does being a volunteer make you feel? One reason that many volunteers stay involved with one-to-one activity and creating options is that they are fed from direct contact with those they are helping. It feels good. When persons are engaged in monitoring, advocacy and confronting, they don't necessarily get the feeding that comes from direct contact. Therefore, it is important for them to get satisfaction from the volunteer experience in other ways. It is particularly important for persons volunteering in the public square to engage with other volunteers. It is also critical for those who lead them to find ways of thanking them. Sometimes people get frustrated and burned out as volunteers because they have not been emotionally satisfied with the experience.

Many of the leaders of the civil rights movement, such as Dr. Martin Luther King, Jr. and Ambassador Andrew Young, started their careers as church pastors. Biblical stories such as the tale of the Good Samaritan were familiar to these leaders, but Ambassador Young recalls a variation on this story. It is told by Jesus in response to the question, who is my neighbor? A lone traveler was going up from Jericho to Jerusalem (Jerusalem is literally "up" from Jericho, being at a much higher altitude. It was a perfect route for ambushes from robbers). So it was that this traveler was set upon, beaten and robbed. Holy people passed the stricken stranger. Finally, a Samaritan, a representative of a group not generally well thought of, stopped and helped. The Samaritan took good care of the wounded man. He put him up at an inn, gave his credit card, so to speak, to the innkeeper, and moved on about his business, promising to pay for everything when he returned. Jesus asked who the neighbor was. The crowd surrounding Jesus responded, "The one who helped." Jesus said, "Go and do likewise." The bottom line of the story is that our neighbors are those in need.

But, what if, as he traveled the road frequently, the Samaritan found the same situation—someone beaten up and robbed, lying in the ditch beside the road? For a while he could keep bandaging up victims, putting them on his donkey, and paying for their lodging while they healed. If he continued to do that, he would certainly continue to wear the title, "Good Samaritan," but sooner or later, as his personal resources gave out, as his credit card reached its limit, he would have to look for other options. He could begin to think about the need for new policies.

In the face of an epidemic of trounced on travelers, the Samaritan could have organized a buddy system for those on the road. He could have put up warning signs for travelers or called city hall to plead for more and better police coverage in this high crime area. Or, perhaps he could have lobbied for stronger laws that would get robbers off the road while simultaneously pursuing a strengthened education system that would give potential robbers other ways of earning a living. He certainly could have told the story to a reporter at the *Jerusalem Journal*. That reporter would then investigate the situation and discover all the other victims and benefactors and tell their stories. A constituency would soon be built to make the road safer. In the framework of Table One, the Samaritan would move from one-to-one actions to public policy advocacy with less direct service impact, but more potential for changing the system of policies that govern the community.

Even the best-informed citizen often asks the question, how can I influence change in the politics of my community? There are a variety of ways that are summarized in Table Two.

The primary course in seeking the transformation of political and economic policy is the vigorous and creative use of the ordinary and legal means available to us as citizens of a nation. Voting in elections is critical, but voting is not enough. Democratic systems offer the possibilities for helping select candidates, for questioning prospective candidates, for participating in campaigns, as well as writing and visiting elected officials. Educating office holders regarding critical matters, by providing facts and other background material, is another possibility. There is finally, also the opportunity to stand for public office or to enter government service directly.

Doing ordinary things in extraordinary ways begins with gaining access to elected officials and their staff by building long term relationships through communicating. Building relationships in the public square is like building relationships in other settings. As human beings, we relate to one another in a variety of ways to accomplish goals. To be human is to be political. Remember, we are all politicians. As we said earlier, politics is everywhere—in our families, schools, neighborhoods, places of work, and even our places of worship. Public officials and their staff are just like us. We relate to them the way we relate to others. Political skills are interpersonal skills. Always remember that there are three keys to influencing public leaders: Relationships, relationships, relationships!

But, before we go about building those relationships, we need to know what we want to accomplish. We need to begin to think and act strategically. Most folks try to be players in the public square by beginning with tactics. Tactics are short-term activities that get you where you want to go. Strategic thinking and acting defines where you want to go. Strategic thinking and acting involves knowing your destination. Tactical thinking tells you how you will get to your destination. Most of us do not start out on a trip unless we know where we are going. When we get to the edge of town, it makes all the difference in the world whether we are going to the

TABLE 7.2

Ways to Influence Change
1. Voting and Campaign Support—volunteering and contributions (Be sure to register first)
2. Influencing Policy—Contacting Representatives: E-mail, Phone call, Letter, Visit
3. Attending public meetings, Coalition building
4. Serving on Boards, Commissions, and Committees
5. Lobbying, Petitions, and Recall
6. Litigation
7. Protest and Confrontation (Using the media)
8. Campaigning for Office

mountains or the beach. Effective players in the public square know where they want to go. What issue or piece of legislation is most important?

Before we start building relationships with public officials and their staff, we also need to know the components of a decision that any public official makes. Envision a pie. One slice of the pie is core value. All public officials have core values. No matter what anybody else says or does, they will not violate their core values. For example, one member of Congress was a former actor whose core values included protecting the First Amendment right of free speech. Another slice of the pie is "significant others," staff, colleagues, trusted friends, and so on. All public officials are highly dependent on information shared by those they trust. All public officials are educated beyond their intelligence. That does not mean they are stupid. It means that they have to know so much about so many things that they cannot possibly know about everything they have to vote on. Another slice of the decision pie is special interest groups—the dreaded lobby. If you agree with them, they are an interest group. If you do not agree with them, they are a lobby. There is a place for interest groups in the public policy process. There are groups that do know a lot about particular issues because they deal with those issues every day. The largest part of the decision pie is constituents. What do my constituents think? Public officials are constantly trying to find out where their constituency is. That makes communicating points of view with public officials critically important.

How do we give input into public decisions? First of all, we need to realize that our task is not to convince public officials. No one has ever been convinced by anyone of anything. People give input to others. That input may be used in helping form a decision, but the decision is internal to the person deciding. Our task is to relate to public officials as effective communicators giving input into public decisions. All effective communication, whether verbal or written, has two parts. The first part is recognizing where the other person is. The second part is clearly stating where we are. In communicating with others, particularly in stressful situations, we tend to do either the first part or the second part. That tendency is really part of the old flight or fight reaction to stressful situations. Some of us, when threatened or under stress (and communicating with public officials can be both) flee by always recognizing the other's position but never saying where we are. When we do that, we never get anywhere. Others of us tend to respond by always stating what we want without regard to the other person's point of view. If we keep doing that long enough, we will get into a fight. It does take practice to put the two parts of effective communication together. The people we communicate with are our fellow citizens and have the right to their opinions. We are also citizens and have the right to our opinion. Remember, our task is not to convince but to communicate.

Being an effective communicator does not mean always getting what we want. Sometimes it means opening up the possibility for compromise. Important public decisions always have multiple points of view represented. We want to make sure that our point of view is represented in the mix. As we take our political skills into the public square in order to make sure our point of view is represented as decisions are made, we use two forms of communication—direct and indirect. Direct communication involves letter writing, telephoning, visiting, attending town hall meetings, and so forth. Indirect communication involves writing letters to the editor, submitting opinion editorial or "op ed" pieces to newspapers, calling talk shows, media coverage, communicating with people who know people. Indirect communication helps form the backdrop, the general sense of where the public is on an issue.

The general rule for direct communication is: That which takes the most care and time to do has the greatest impact. In terms of written communication, a well thought-out letter generally has much more impact than a petition with hundreds of signatures. A well-dressed petitioner can stake out a shopping mall in the Midwest on a Saturday morning and get several hundred signatures in favor of saving alligators in Lake Michigan. Receivers of petitions (with the exception of signatures needed to put a referendum on a ballot), will be polite but not swayed. The nagging question is always, "Do these folks really know what they are signing?"

On the other hand, a well-written letter shows a public official that the sender really does know what he or she is writing about.

An effective letter to a public official includes:

1. A salutation. Say something nice, even if only to recognize that the official has a tough job.

2. Your credentials. There is no one who is a greater authority on you than you. You are first of all a constituent (which translates into voter). Then you are a parent, student, homemaker, minister, teacher, businessperson, and so on.

3. A message. Clearly state your issue, the reasons for your concern, and what position you would like the official to take on the issue.

4. A request for response. Ask the official to reply. Most people never ask for a reply.

5. A final word of appreciation. Thank the official for the work that she or he is doing.

Effective letters are one page and tightly focused on one issue or piece of legislation. It is generally best not to refer to a group that has asked you to write. Avoid triggered communication. Elected officials are looking for a broad-based consensus among constituents.

Letter writing can be planned and organized in a way that does not seem to be triggered. A letter-writing party is fun. Gather folks for dessert and coffee. Explain the issue at hand. Have plenty of all kinds of stationery and writing instruments. Encourage participants to write in their own words. Stamp the letters with different stamps. Collect the letters. Over the next week, put the letters in different mail boxes. Lots of letters can be generated without them having a triggered (someone told me to write) feel.

A visit to a public official has the same flow as a letter. When you greet the public official and/or his or her staff, say something nice. Introduce yourself using the same guidelines as letter writing. You are a constituent (the magic word). You do such and such as an occupation. You are visiting because of your concern about such and such an issue or piece of legislation. Ask the official where she or he stands on the issue or legislation. Thank the official and/or staff for the time spent with you. An optimum number of visitors is three. One person focuses on the official and is the prime spokesperson for the group while another person focuses on staff and the third person acts as timekeeper. Be sensitive to the official's schedule. A visit will probably last no more than 15 minutes. If the official or the staff person wants to continue the conversation, they will let you know. Nothing will damage your visit more than overstaying your welcome.

Phone calls have the greatest impact if there is a large number of them and if they are made prior to an important decision. It is easier to call than it is to write. Writing is preferable, however, if you have the time. As noted, most elected officials have certain issues that are so important to them that they will risk their careers for those issues. Most of the time, however, elected officials vote for what they believe is in the best interests of their constituents—the common good. A vote in Congress or at the state house or city hall often means that the official has determined what the majority of his or her constituents want. But, since most constituents never write, call, or visit, officials often rely on indirect communication to get a fix on their constituency. Whatever influences public opinion will ultimately influence public officials.

It is important to get to know persons in the media. Who covers the issues that concern you? Often we send press releases to faceless addresses and wonder why the paper doesn't send a reporter. If we know the reporter, our press releases might find their way to the top of the stack on his or her desk. The first thing that most elected officials and staff do in the morning is read the paper. A timely letter to the editor can help form opinion. One of the staff persons in most offices of elected public officials clips letters to the editor every morning and places them in the center of the official's desk.

When you write a letter to the editor, make your opinion clear from the beginning. Don't try to combine opinions several issues in one letter. Keep sentences, paragraphs, and letters short. The more concise the letter is, the more likely it is to be published. Make sure you have all the facts, names, dates, and quotations correct and cite sources if possible. Don't worry about having to be a professional writer. Your own reasoned judgment communicates better than well-turned phrases. Write about whatever you think is important. Letters can inform, make suggestions, react to news or other letters, critique, and say thank you. As with writing a letter to a public official, say something nice about the paper. Papers perform an important role by encouraging moral discourse.

An often overlooked form of indirect communication is passing information through those who know the official you are communicating with. If you get to know staff well and are trusted by them, they may tell you who the elected official looks to for advice. Biographies of elected officials are also good leads as to who knows whom. Is the official active in the Scouts or Rotary? Where does he or she worship? What schools did she or he attend? Get a biography from the official's office. Another form of indirect communication is looking at the list of people who contribute to the elected official's campaign. For local offices, you can obtain the list of contributors from your county elections office. For statewide and congressional offices, the secretary of state in your state will have a list. These lists are now computerized in most counties and states, so you can go on line to find out the information. You might be surprised to see who is on the list. You just might know someone who is a contributor. Those who contribute to an elected official are not buying votes. The cynicism abroad often makes that incorrect assumption. What contributions sometimes do is provide access. Contributions indicate support, and we tend to know those who support us.

After we know why we are advocating, what we are advocating for in the long run, and how to advocate, then we need to make sure we know the lay of the land. Who are the staff persons who work with the officials whose vote we want? All elected officials whether they are a city council member, a county commissioner, or a U.S. senator, do two things. They form public policy and they provide constituency service, helping solve problems with the government. They have staff which helps them do those two jobs. Some staffs are small. State representatives may have one person who performs both duties. Other staffs are larger. A congressional office may have up to twenty people. Get to know staff!!! Get to know those who relate to the issue and/or agency you are interested in.

There is often a short jump from communicating with public officials to being involved in the election process. Sometimes the journey toward being senior staff with a U.S. representative begins with putting up a yard sign. People can be involved in the election process by helping candidates whom they identify with or by running for office.

There are other ways to influence change in your community that are summarized in Table Two. Local governments, in particular, depend upon a variety of boards, commissions, and committees in order to get the work of the city or county done. A glance at the web site of the City of Atlanta government indicates that there are more than fifty of these citizen groups that range literally from A (the Atlanta/Fulton County Library Board of Trustees) to Z (the Zoning Review Board). Appointments to these are usually made by the mayor's office or a city council member. Local officials look to those they know among their constituents with whom the official has a relationship. Anyone who has followed some of the steps described above and formed a relationship with a public official or staff member is in a good position to volunteer for a board, commission, or committee.

Occasionally, citizens become discontented with their elected officials and wish to express their anger by removing the person from office. Local requirements for recalling an elected public official vary, but, in general a certain percentage of the registered voters in the locality must sign a recall petition. When the required number of signatures is obtained and verified, a special election is held in order to recall the elected public official and remove the person from office before the completion of the regular term of office. Getting the required number of signatures from registered voters is often a difficult and time consuming process. In cases of corruption or malfeasance in office, a recall petition may be used along with possible litigation. Rather than go through the process of a recall, it is often better to organize opposition to an office holder and be prepared for the next election.

The United States is sometimes described as a litigious society, as we often resolve conflicts in the courtroom. Litigation can play a role in influencing change within a community. Individuals who feel that decisions by their local government adversely affect them have the right to bring lawsuits in order to force changes in policies. Businesses, neighborhood organizations, and individuals sue their local government and its agencies when they feel their interests have been harmed. The legal process can be expensive for an individual, but it can be used to bring attention to an issue regardless of the outcome.

In 1960, a group of college students in Greensboro, North Carolina, began a process of confronting the segregated policies of businesses and local government by peacefully sitting down at a lunch counter and refusing to leave when they were refused service. Other groups of students repeated this form of protest in towns and cities throughout the south, eventually leading to the passage of the 1964 Civil Rights Act that required the desegregation of restaurants, hotels, and other businesses engaged in interstate commerce. Successful protests such as these follow certain patterns. First, the issue that is the target of the protest must be important and in need of attention. Next, there must be careful planning and organization. During the civil rights movement, a network of organizations emerged including nonprofit groups such as the Southern Christian Leadership Conference, the Congress of Racial Equality, and the Student Non-Violent Coordinating Committee. Often the leaders studied the nonviolent principles used by Gandhi in freeing India from British colonial rule. In the struggle for national independence in India, as well as the civil rights movement in the United States, nonviolence was an important strategy for making change. Even when faced with fire hoses, vicious dogs, and the "billy clubs" of local and state police, Martin Luther King, Jr. and his associates in the movement met the force of violence with the strategy of nonviolent resistance. The demonstrators were willing to face arrest for their refusal to stop the peaceful protest marches. But, they were ultimately successful in bringing attention to their cause and in changing policies. Anyone using protest and confrontation would do well to study the nonviolent tactics of Gandhi and King to achieve political change.

There is one other important way to influence change in a community that good citizens ought to consider—running for office. In election terms, the desire to run for office can be described as having a "fire in your belly." People who decide to run for office have to really want to run. In order to go through what a person goes through in a campaign, running for office requires a steadfastness of purpose forged from an inner desire that pushes a person into the public arena. A candidate simply has to run for office. He or she can do no other. Often candidates find a place to run by looking at an area of government in which they have been involved. One member of a board of education ran for office after she had been involved in the Parent Teacher Association. She came to see that she could make education policy decisions as well as and maybe even better than those she knew on the school board. A county commissioner decided to run after having successfully led neighborhood opposition to a zoning decision. Sometimes circumstances thrust a candidate onto the public stage. Whatever the motivation, running for office yourself is one way to answer the question, why doesn't the city council care about the important issues that really matter to me?

How do you choose the issues on which you want to work? This chapter has made a case for beginning with process and moving to issues. It is important to know why we are doing what we are doing, who we are doing it with and how we are going to do it before we start. We've also add to our practical political skill bag. Now let us turn to the identification of issues in the public square that merit our attention. Only a few years ago, members of Congress and their staff members were made aware of the tragedy of famine in Ethiopia. During a six-month period, one congressional office received about fifty letters asking for the congressman to make U.S. aid available to Ethiopia. During that same six-month period, there were over six hundred letters complaining about airport noise. This is not to say that the people who complained about the airport were wrong or bad. It simply illustrates the point that rarely in the public square do we find persons advocating on behalf of someone else, particularly if that someone else is a child, and a foreign child at that. One of the realities of the U.S. Congress is that assignments on committees that have to do with things like providing foreign aid and caring for children domestically or internationally are not the most popular. This does not mean that representatives and senators do not care about such issues. It simply points to the reality of a representative democracy. Children can't vote, and if it's a foreign child, the child's parents can't vote. The simple truth is those who make their voices heard often get policy formed to their liking. In a representative democracy, the squeaky wheel does get the grease.

In order for those who cannot speak or who speak very softly to be heard, people like you and me—who are also voters and constituents of public officials—must speak. By speaking, I'm talking about the sometimes overwhelming work of organizing people, writing letters, visiting representatives, working for candidates, litigation, protesting, even running for office.

How do you choose the issues on which to work? One way to choose issues to work on is to see what others are working on and join forces as allies. As you choose your issue, remember to focus. One issue or piece of legislation is great. Two issues or pieces of legislation are okay. Three issues or pieces of legislation are so-so. More than that is a disaster. People will often shotgun issues and therefore are ineffective on any single issue. Pick issues that are winnable and easily defined. If you cannot explain the issue to a person in the brief time that it takes an elevator to make a trip up in a major building, (say between thirty and sixty seconds) find another issue to address. That said, sometimes you will select a more complex issue that may also be unwinnable, but it important enough to you to make the effort. Sometimes the issue will be one about which you care passionately since it is part of your core values. Other times, taking on a new issue may provide an opportunity to learn about a policy that you are able to see in a new light.

If the imperative is to participate in the process of making policy decisions in the public square, why do so few people get involved? Perhaps if more people understood how to be good citizens in their community, they would jump into the public square. The biggest barrier to getting involved in the public square is fear of the unknown, of making a mistake, of being out of control, of being overwhelmed. Fear is powerful. Fear takes hold when we begin to do something that we have never done before. The only way to handle the fear associated with doing new things is to begin to do those new things. To show you how you might begin, Jim Watkins tells the following story:

> IN ONE OF MY LESS SANE MOMENTS, WHEN I WAS IN THE ARMY, I VOLUNTEERED TO BE A PARATROOPER. FOR THREE WEEKS WE PRACTICED JUMPING OUT A DOOR AND LANDING AND ROLLING ON THE GROUND UNTIL THOSE ACTIVITIES BECAME AUTOMATIC. I KNEW ALL THE MECHANICS OF JUMPING AND I WANTED TO GET MY WINGS. BUT I STILL HAD TO GO OUT THE DOOR. THERE IS NO FEAR LIKE THAT OF LEAVING THE DOOR OF A PERFECTLY GOOD AIRPLANE!

> AFTER MY FIRST JUMP, I ASKED THE JUMP MASTER, WHO HAD MADE THOUSANDS OF JUMPS, INCLUDING A JUMP INTO NORMANDY IN WORLD WAR II, IF A PERSON EVER GETS OVER THE FEAR OF LEAVING THE DOOR OF THE AIRPLANE. "NO", HE SAID, "AND IF YOU DO, DON'T JUMP."

If you have never written or visited a public official, the thought of doing so will bring anxiety. If you or someone you know has had a thought about running for office, the anxiety produced by that thought may have pushed the possibility back deep down within you or them. If you have thought about working on matters in the public square, perhaps your anxiety has stopped you from tackling the topics. Go on out the door! When you do, you will find that you are not alone.

We hope that you will take the plunge to use your new-found knowledge and skills to be a good citizen in your community.

CHAPTER 7
Participating as a Citizen in your Community

1. Select an example of a one-to-one activity and an example of public policy advocacy. Describe how the two activities differ in terms of their impacts on direct service and on system change.

2. An important tool for influencing policy change is letter writing. Draft a letter to a local elected public official using some of the suggestions provided in the chapter.

3. Compile a list of the boards, commissions, and committees that are an official part of your local government. Describe in a paragraph how the members of one of these groups could influence change in a policy issue affecting your community. How could you become a member of this group?

4. What are some of the strengths and weaknesses of using protest and confrontation as a method of changing policy in your community? Describe an example of this process and its outcome.